Power Up
For Success

Other Controversial Titles From New Falcon Publications

Undoing Yourself With Energized Meditation
Secrets of Western Tantra
The Tree of Lies
    All By Christopher S. Hyatt, Ph.D.
The Enochian World of Aleister Crowley
    By Aleister Crowley, L. M. DuQuette, and C. S. Hyatt
The Way of The Secret Lover
    By Christopher S. Hyatt, Ph.D. and Lon M. DuQuette
Aleister Crowley's Illustrated Goetia: Sexual Evocation
    By C. S. Hyatt, L. M. DuQuette and D. Wilson
Taboo: The Ecstacy of Evil—
   The Psychopathology of Sex and Religion
    By C. S. Hyatt, L. M. DuQuette and G. Ford
Pacts With The Devil
    By S. J. Black and Christopher. S. Hyatt, Ph.D.
Urban Voodoo
    By Christopher. S. Hyatt, Ph.D. and S. J. Black
Equinox of the Gods
Eight Lectures on Yoga
Gems From the Equinox
Little Essays Toward Truth
Heart of the Master
    All By Aleister Crowley
The Psychology of Synergy
Insights
    Both By Dr. Madeleine Singer
Neuropolitique
Info-Psychology
    Both By Timothy Leary, Ph.D.
Zen Without Zen Masters
A Handful of Zen
    Both By Camden Benares
The Complete Golden Dawn System of Magic
Healing Energy, Prayer and Relaxation
    All By Israel Regardie

And to get your free catalog of *all* of our titles, write to:
NEW FALCON PUBLICATIONS
Catalog Dept.
655 East Thunderbird
PHOENIX, AZ 85022 U.S.A.

Power Up For Success

By
Dr. Madeleine Singer

1993
NEW FALCON PUBLICATIONS
PHOENIX, ARIZONA U.S.A.

COPYRIGHT © 1993 DR. MADELEINE SINGER

All rights reserved. No part of this book, in part or in whole, may be reproduced, transmitted, or utilized, in any form or by any means, electronic or mechanical, including photocopying, recording, or by any information storage and retrieval system, without permission in writing from the publisher, except for brief quotations in critical articles, books and reviews.

International Standard Book Number: 1-56184-070-X

First Edition 1993

NEW FALCON PUBLICATIONS
655 East Thunderbird
Phoenix, Arizona 85022 U.S.A.
(602) 246-3546

Table of Contents

ENERGY DYNAMICS

Introduction 10
Building Blocks 11
The Pendulum Effect 12
Levels Of Energy 13
Aura 14
Intuition 16
Effects Of Energy 17
Various Energy Fields 18
Magnetism 20
Time\Space 21
Universal Laws 22
The Hologram 24
Entropy 26
Energy Exchange 27
Evolution 29
Emotions 30

EXERCISES

Energy Fields 32
Getting Results 33
Feeling Energy 34
Energy Shield 35
Sensing Energy 36
Sensing Energy Fields 37
Breath And Relaxation Techniques 38
    Basic Breathing
    Abdominal Breathing
Relaxation Techniques 39
Glass Body 40
Seeing The Electro-Magnetic Field 41

BREAKING THE STRESS BARRIER

Go For It! 44
Stressors 45
Stress Syndrome 46
Managing Stress 48
Positive Thoughts 50

Physical Reactions 52
Holistic Vs. Traditional 53
    Holistic Practitioner
    Traditional Practitioner
Symptoms Of Stress 55
Benefits Of Relaxation Techniques 57
Reaction To Stress 58
Sounding Board 60
Tips To Ease Tension 62
What Do You Really Want? 63

EXERCISES

Resistance 66
Affirming Change 68
Positive Futures 69
Confidence 70
Stressors 71
Accentuate The Positive 72
Stress Reducers 73
Schedule 74

FROM BURNOUT TO SUCCESS

Health And Balance 76
Burnout 78
Strategies For Accessing Mood Changes 80
Steps For Success 81
Strategy For Success 83
Ladder Of Success 84
Creative Thinking 86
Your True Character 88
Developing New Ideas 89
Metaphors 90
Taking Risks 91
Self-Esteem 93
Process To Bolster Self-Esteem 94
Pathways For Success 95
    Seven Winning Behaviors You Need For Success
    Six Key Beliefs For Success That All Successful
      People Know

—RELATIONSHIPS—THE MATING GAME

Four Misconceptions Of Love 100
Strengthening Your Intimate Relationship 102
Three Techniques For Making Your Relationship Great 104
Creating The Relationship You Deserve 106
Eliminating Fear 110
Characteristics For Happiness 112
Evaluating Your Relationship 114
Co-Creating 117
Five Common Mind-Sets 118

THERAPEUTIC TOUCH

Why Therapeutic Touch Works 120
Kirlian Photography 122
History Of Touch 123
Case Studies 125
Concepts 130
Benefits Of Touch 131
Characteristics Of Colored Light 132
Process Of Therapeutic Touch 133
    Centering
    Assessment
    Unruffling
    Energy Transference
    Stopping
Disrupting Disease 137
The Brain 138
Creative Energy 139
Holographics 140
Replicating Cells 141
Healers 142

EXERCISES

Testing The Human Energy Field 144
Breathing Techniques 145
Relaxation Techniques 147
Intensifying Energy Fields 148
Shielding 149

TIDBITS FOR EFFECTIVE LIVING

Speak To Your Brain 152
Comfort Vs. Risk 153
Excellence 154
Smile, You're On Candid Camera 155
Success 156
Cells That Think 157
Truth Or Fiction 158
Goal Setting 159
Priorities 160
Internal Rhythms 161
Blame 162
Peace And Contentment 163
Winners Vs. Losers 164
Clear Thinking 166
The Energizer 167
Shifting Moods 168
Unlimited Power 169
Behavior Vs. Feelings 170
Switching Emotions 171
Conditioning 172
Dynamics Of Change 174
Belief Systems 175
Process For Change 176
Facts And Opinions 177
Present Time 179
Awareness 180
Be True To Yourself 181
Relaxation Vs. Tension 183
Mood Changers 184
Deep Breathing 185
Changing Perspectives 186
Thinking For Health 187
Symbols For Growth 188
Responsibility 189
Calmness And Power 190

About the Author 191

ENERGY DYNAMICS

INTRODUCTION

Everyone's purpose in life changes from one priority to another. One goal, however, that should always remain constant is the ability to become and stay the master of one's own being. Too often that ability is surrendered to someone or something else and a victim's role takes the place of strength and well-being. My entire professional career has been devoted to showing people how to maintain balance, power, and self-esteem. This book is a compilation of knowledge from my workshops to show you how to actually do healing, direct energy to attract what you want, have great relationships and maintain them, go from burnout to success and self-esteem, and how to effortlessly become the best you can be.

The first step is to recognize negativity and weakness; even more important is for you to know how to change them into positivity and strength. My methods are aimed at doing just that. Common sense is the key. Positive thinking goes just so far; but coupling it with faith and positive action guarantees that your results will improve tremendously. When this is accomplished, a mind-body connection is the result. Read each chapter, practice the exercises and become the *YOU* that you wish. Reality is whatever you perceive it to be. This book will guide and direct you for your own personal evolution.

BUILDING BLOCKS

Everything in the entire universe can be reduced to energy. No matter what the object—animate or inanimate—it can be broken down into molecules, atoms, electrons, neutrons, protons, and now it is even being further reduced into positrons and quarks. All of this is considered to be energy. Science and religion have some of the same basic concepts; only the semantics differ. For instance, religion talks of the divine or spirit being everything; science uses the term atoms instead. Energy *is* everything, not *in* everything. You are a person and not a cup because of the configuration of your molecular structure. Energy cannot be contained within your skin so it billows forth. This is called an aura or your electromagnetic field. Measurements have shown that the human energy field has fluid-like motion. When it is charged, minute particles move together in clouds and are called plasmas. They are considered to be in a state between energy and matter and are therefore called "bioplasma."

THE PENDULUM EFFECT

Science now thinks of man's consciousness as a level of energy. If this is so, then energy could be graphically displayed by a sine curve (one that rises above and below a base line.) All modes of energy demonstrate a continual fluctuation between extreme values above and below this base line and the energy creates an oscilloscope. It is difficult to conceive that life's energy should differ from all other energy forms and that it should not oscillate or pass from one state called "life" to another called "death" (It is within this state that the spirit is aligned with the absolute) and back again.

Reality, as we know it, could be likened to a pendulum. Our consciousness is the swing of the pendulum as it swings from left to right, and back again from right to left. This could be called "tangible reality." It is the world as we know it. The pause at the top of the swing before it resumes in its opposite direction is a moment of complete rest. This is the moment of eternity. It is the opening into the absolute and brings the consciousness into another dimension of thought and into the realm of the universal energy bank. It is within this space that we can manipulate and tap into various frequencies that are usually veiled to us. It is in this altered state that Mozart, Einstein, Keats and many other such geniuses achieved some of their inspiration. In this sphere, their consciousness was in conjunction with a different realm of thinking. Meditation is one method to lengthen this pause of the pendulum's swing (moment of eternity) and allows the body to resonate with the frequencies of the absolute. It is in this state that creativity and intuition become natural.

LEVELS OF ENERGY

There are several levels of existence above the physical. There is an electric layer that goes beyond the atmosphere of the earth. The vibrations are so high that we hardly call them matter. They can be considered music since they vibrate in the etheric layer and resonate with a definite musical sound. Pythagoras taught about the music of the spheres. He realized that each particle vibrates and creates two things through the vibrations—light and sound. Today we have an instrument to show that sound is light and that light is sound. Through electronics we can show that each vibration has its own color, its own reflection of light, and its own sound. In studying the principle of vibration, one realizes that the higher the vibration, the more subtle the mass; the lower the vibration, the more solid the mass. Therefore, the physical body is a much slower vibration than the etheric or subtle energy bodies. The faster the vibration, the quicker the manifestation of what that vibration represents. That is why it seems to take a while until the result of our action comes to fruition. In the spirit or etheric layers, the effect happens much faster and could be instantaneous. Take this as an example: A person's life is full of wrong-doings and he may or may not *seem* to get his comeuppance in this lifetime. When he dies, his spirit goes to a place where the same magnetic frequencies that he radiates are also resonating. This, in a religious term, could be considered Hell. When a righteous person dies, his spirit is attracted to another stratosphere where his same vibrations are radiating and he could be considered going to Heaven. In these cases, the results happen immediately. When there is no dense matter, the effects are immediate. These two people have created their own Heaven or Hell.

All matter can be called spirit. Truth is pure spirit. Each transformation is a learning experience. If you think your way is better, prove it by *being* better, not by *talking* better.

AURA

Since everything is made up of energy, everything has an aura. Therefore, everything and everybody impact everything else. Every object is in constant motion as energy is always moving. We consider people, animals, rocks or buildings as being dense matter and negate the fact that they are made up of energy and are in motion. The atoms, in what we consider dense matter, are moving too quickly or too slowly for our range of vision; but certain biological frequency rates can be measured by various machines such as an EKG, EEG, or various others which will measure our brain waves, heart rate, pulse rate, etc. One of the newer machines is called the SQUID (Superconducting Quantum Interference Device) which can measure infinitesimally weak magnetic fields. The tangible world is not a collection of moving objects, but movement itself. It is the movement which constitutes the objects that appear to us. This movement is a continued and infinitely rapid succession of flashes of energy. We are composed of frequencies that operate at certain levels. Think of the terms that we use: She is energetic—meaning she pushes out energy. "She is withdrawn." What she has withdrawn is her energy. "He is depressed." What is depressed is that person's energy. These terms are common and all deal with what we feel and how we process.

Energy can be felt and is constantly being transferred. Our electro-magnetic field is generally three to six feet around us. If we are standing near a person within that vicinity, the two fields are intertwined. Have you ever been next to a person and had your mood change? What happened is that you picked up his vibration and made it your own. When you have stepped into a room full of people, you can sense what we call "vibes." In actuality it is the energy output of the people that you are sensing. If it is a party, you can call it good vibes or bad vibes and act accordingly. Take this scenario: You have had the best day. Everything has gone great and you feel on top. You now walk into a room full of people who have had a mediocre day. What kind of vibes do you feel? Say I have had a terrible day. Everything has gone wrong and I walk into that same room at the same time. What kind of reaction would I have? You would feel that the energy of these people are pulling you down since your energy is so much higher at this point and I would feel that it would be a pick-me-up as they are the best sensations that I had encountered all day. It's the same energy output, yet a very different reaction as both of our perspectives are coming from two different places. It is not what is being said. It is the energy that is exuding from these individuals that impacts us.

INTUITION

Ever have a person saying all the "right" words, yet your gut feeling is saying something quite the opposite? What you are receiving is the energy output that is telling you something else. When we go along with our instincts, we are usually correct. Too often we don't trust it and go with our intellect, only to find that it was the intuitive that was correct. People never deceive us with their words or actions. It is entirely our fault if we cannot cut through to our instincts to read, feel or sense what their energy is actually telling us. Energy is the life force that exists in every cell. We have the power to control, rather than allow situations and people to control us. Since energy cannot be destroyed, it can be directed and harnessed to serve us. Too often we blame others for our failures. It is important to take credit for our successes as well as learning from our mistakes.

EFFECTS OF ENERGY

Hospitals now recognize that everything in the room affects the patient and administrators are being more careful as to what color the room is painted and how it could change illness into health. All-spectrum lighting is put into most places as the frequencies make the people feel better. When it was all fluorescent lighting, people were tired and lethargic because some of the frequencies that should be contained in the lighting were missing. This created a certain deficiency of energy within the body as it could not absorb those necessary rays from the lights. The more we are aware of energy, the more we can control how it affects us. Most energies are so subtle that they impact us without our knowledge. Television frequencies, refrigerators, micro-waves, lights, sounds and so forth all are part of our daily lives and can affect our health drastically. The human body is a matrix of oscillating fields of energy which affects and is influenced by outside fields such as weather patterns, tides, the sun or moon, or can be influenced by broadcasting fields of radio and television waves.

VARIOUS ENERGY FIELDS

The electro-magnetic fields making up and shaping our bodies serve to hold our atoms and molecules together. We are surrounded and permeated by several fields: the isoelectric static field of the planet; the electrostatic fields of the earth; the electro-magnetic field, which has a wide spectrum, ranging from the slow wave caused by disturbances in the atmosphere, through the spectrum of visible light into the ultraviolet and higher frequency radiation; the gravitational fields of the earth, moon, and neighboring planets and the sun; the electro-magnetic fields caused by humans and the different broadcasting fields of the networks. This explains why there is no division between the observer and the observed, as both merge and interpenetrate aspects of one reality which is indivisible. View the world in terms of a universal flux of events and processes. Separateness is illusory. Botanist Rupert Sheldrake proposed that these fields are morphogenetic. As an example he stated that rats in one laboratory learned a maze and after that other rats anywhere in the world learned that maze faster. Another instance is when some monkeys started washing their food in the water and other monkeys around the world started doing the same. These are two cases that proved once a thought has been thought, it can be communicated to others. This can be why an important discovery can be made simultaneously by several people working independently in different areas of the world.

Everything is a frequency. Emotions are frequencies. The emotions of peace, harmony, contentment and love have been scientifically measured by machines to have a light, fast ray. The emotions of hate, anger and hostility have a heavy, slow wave length. Every organ, muscle, tissue and cell of our body vibrate at a certain frequency rate. We talk about having "highs and lows." Those are the wave lengths that can be graphed to show how the body is vibrating. The body can spin faster when it is composed of lighter and faster frequencies. A person becomes this combination of fast, light frequencies when calmness, stability and contentment become more and more the norm. The slower, heavier vibrations then spin off as they cannot keep up the faster pace. The result is that some of these negative emotions are then modified and the person can get back to a stabilized position in a faster period of time.

Some people can be considered "energy sappers." We have all come in contact with these people. They talk incessantly, quickly and seem to drain our energy. When they leave, we feel as if a tornado had come by and left us exhausted. The best way to deal with them is to recognize who they are and protect ourselves by the use of a shield. Look in the exercise portion to learn how to do this. Detach and view the situation as you would a movie. Then you will not get emotionally involved with the other person's hyperactivity.

MAGNETISM

You are magnetic energy and magnetically draw to you whatever you need. You form this energy into what you desire through your pictures, thought patterns, feelings and perceptions of experiences. The subconscious brings you what you have stored in your energy field. As your thoughts are of youth, health and beauty, the cells you reproduce become more whole and perfect. As you repeat positive statements, they go down into the subconscious, take form in the body, and the body expresses a positive attitude. Creative energy is passive. You mold it according to your thoughts and feelings. Your subconscious mind works from knowing the end result and uses the information stored in the mind and body. You set causes into motion that produce effects. The quality of your job, relationships, health, etc. reflect and reinforce the belief systems you hold in your consciousness.

If you don't like what is being pulled to you, you must lift your vibrations to attract better situations. Relaxation techniques or meditation should be done at least twice a day. This centers you for clearer thinking. The exercises at the end of this chapter will show you how to do this.

Realize that even the best of the psychics are still bound to filter the truth through their own veil of experiences. Never give total control to someone else. Utilize their opinion as a second opinion or as another option; but always finalize the result yourself.

All material substances are impregnated with past and present experiences. Furniture as well as the rooms in our house are ingrained with the quality of emotional contact to which it has been exposed. If you take the furniture to another place, it will still be projecting the frequencies of past experiences until the emotionality of events change. If you had a stressful relationship, you will feel those types of vibrations from the furniture.

TIME\SPACE

Physical matter is the world of positive space\time. This is electrical in nature. Energies that vibrate beyond the speed of light are referred to as the world of negative space\time and are magnetic. These energies tend toward negative entropy. That is, the energies of the etheric bodies have qualities which move cellular systems toward states of higher order and organization. The removal of this negative-entropic tendency following the dissipation of the etheric vehicle at death is the reason that the body decays after dying. Once the organizing influence of the etheric body has dissipated, the body follows a positively entropic downward spiral of cellular breakdown.

UNIVERSAL LAWS

There are certain laws of the universe. The more we know about these laws, the closer aligned we will be to reality. Everything else is just our idea of reality. Changes in nature are little leaps. There are no smooth continuous movements of anything. Energy is radiated, emitted and absorbed in spurts. Einstein said, "Energy has mass and mass represents energy." Therefore, mass and energy are different forms of the same thing. The law of conservation states that a quantity of something never changes. The total amount of energy in the universe has been and always will be the same. By expanding our awareness to include functions which normally lie beyond its parameters (controlling the autonomic nervous system—heart rate, brain waves, pulse rate), we can experience certain processes that were not in our awareness before and experience a timelessness and oneness with the universe. The brain is more energetic when it is less active. At the lower frequencies (alpha or theta) the brain receives and stores more information. Time is a sequence of motions that we developed to explain our perception of change. No two people experience time the same way. Different interpretations of time can come from the person's inner clock. If their clocks run much faster, the internal perception of time is interpreted as "running out of time." Others have all the time in the world and time can "stand still." The body is a fluctuation of information and derives its information from other fields of energy. The body is a field of ideas that makes interpretations to the mind. There is no space and time difference. We normally perceive and think in terms of a separation and compartmentalization of this oneness. When you are thirsty, it happens simultaneously throughout the body and does not happen in a linear sequence. There is no absolute time as there is no single time that is exact for all observers. When you are flying in outer space, time and space are one. In our sensory reality, time is divided into past, present, and future. With this notion, time can prevent energy and information exchange between two individual objects. By contrast it can be thought of as time without divisions: past, present, and future are illusory. Sequences of action exist, but these happen in multi-levels of the present.

With this hypothesis, time cannot prevent energy of information exchange between two individual objects since the division of time does not exist and everything resides in the "eternal now." You are able to relate to the levels and frequencies that your electro-magnetics can tune into. The focus is not with particles as units of energy, but with the patterns of energy flow. We have become used to having a beginning, middle, and end so that we can predict probable ends for events. It is rather disconcerting to think of reading these patterns without a past, present, and future, but all at once.

Einstein perceived that there was nothing at rest anywhere in the universe—that all particles (atoms, planets, galaxies, or ourselves) were moving, but these movements could be described only in relation to one another. Our calendar sense of time was linked to the movement of the objects we call space. Einstein demonstrated that clocks attached to any moving system ran slower than when they were stationary. For example, a space traveler would come back younger than when he started the journey if the elements were right. He believed that the universe was not a machine that looked and operated the same with or without a human; that time and space were constructs of the human mind; and that relativity of all things changed according to the nature and situation of the human observer.

THE HOLOGRAM

The hologram theory postulates that each cell of an organism contains the entire organism. If one could dissect and magnify one cell of you enough times, all of you would be contained within it—the same way that the seed of a tree contains the entire tree. According to this holographic theory, if we are each parts of a larger whole—that is if our minds and bodies are holograms within the larger hologram of the universe—then there is no transmission problem between energy patterns as any and all information is already within us. If this premise is correct, then we would be in a reality in which everything interconnects and interfaces with us. Then all energy does indeed impact us and we impact everything else. The manifested reality of mind and matter is a fraction of the whole or infinite reality. The mind limits consciousness so that the mind may have finite experiences. Individual consciousness is a partial expression of cosmic consciousness. In essence because both of these are consciousness, they are indivisible. The two are usually separated by subjectivity and cause us to have limited vision. The energy of our unconscious can touch many various levels that our consciousness veils. In order to have entry into these frequencies, the brain waves must slow down to alpha or theta. That is best accomplished in our dream state or through relaxation techniques.

It is known from the optics of holograms that all the elements of the hologram contain complete information about the objects portrayed in the hologram. If we illuminate just a small area of the hologram, the image will appear fuzzy: it will have a low definition. If we illuminate a larger area of the same hologram, the image will appear much sharper. Therefore, people with higher levels of consciousness will intuitively view and deal with past, present, or future events more accurately than those who are not as evolved.

The more matter is enlarged with a big microscope, the less you would find until you would end up with a void permeated by pulsating energy fields. If we should slow down the pulsation of our energy fields, we get back to the absolute where there is no motion, no time and no matter. The absolute is pure consciousness combined with intelligence and pure potential.

ENTROPY

Entropy is a term which describes the state of disorder of a system. The greater the disorder, the higher the entropy; the more ordered the system, the lower the entropy. Crystals represent the lowest entropic states possible. Most processes in the physical universe are believed to head toward increasing positive entropy; that is, given time, everything tends to fall apart. The life-force seems to possess negative entropic characteristics. This energy moves biological systems toward increasing levels of cellular order and self-organization. This is the organizing life-force which maintains and sustains the growth of the physical body. At death, this energy dissolves and returns to the free energy of the environment. The potential for a truly preventative medicine lies within a scanner that could detect illness at the etheric level prior to it becoming manifest in the physical body. Cancer is a prime example of a disorder in which cellular replication has gone awry. If the etheric pattern could be changed, then it would probably not manifest at the physical level.

ENERGY EXCHANGE

There is always some degree of an energy exchange with everything from the broad spectrum of the mineral kingdom to man. Consciousness is the capacity of a system to respond to stimuli. Consciousness resides in all matter to a greater or lesser extent. There is nothing that is absolutely conscious or unconscious. In man, consciousness exists as self-consciousness which makes him different from all other forms of existing consciousness. Man can perceive his relationship to the universe and the part he can play. The atom has consciousness because it can respond to stimuli. Since all physical reality is constructed of atoms, all mass contains a percentage of consciousness. This percentage varies in quantity and in quality according to the different evolutionary levels. The quality of consciousness defines the intelligence of the response. The quantity of consciousness defines the number of responses it is capable of. A rock will contain less consciousness than a dog. This entails the rock's lesser degree of control over its environment, fewer possible responses, and less free will. The higher we move on the evolutionary scale, the more control or manipulation we have for creating our environment. Human consciousness can be taught to expand and to learn how to interact with the whole spectrum of realities. This is what the expansion of one's consciousness is about. As we evolve, intuition becomes more the norm and knowledge comes in a nonlinear way. Symbology and images take the place of words. When we are in a relaxed or altered state, the mind resonates with a higher level frequency and is able to absorb information to which we are not normally attuned. It is usually difficult to stop our mind from chatting and thinking. Try to stop the thinking process by closing your eyes and listening to what is going on inside. Follow a thought back to its origin. It may be felt as a little impulse. This implies that we are thinking on a level on which thought is not yet formulated. Therefore, our brain is not the *source* of thought, but a *thought amplified*. It is the function of our brain to amplify the signal for us so that we can put it into a useful form. Free will is built into the system of evolved creatures so they can become co-creators. We choose our own paths; but once chosen, each path has its end result predetermined to fit in with the general event matrix. An event matrix equals the field patterns of diverse shapes within time and space to fit into the entire holographic pattern of your particular path.

EVOLUTION

There is a concept of time which has been referred to as the "eternal now" where past, present, and future may exist simultaneously but in different vibrational time frames. It is possible that by shifting the frequency focus of one's consciousness, one may be able to tune into specific time frames outside of the present.

Imagine that the universe is a big black ball that contains everything there is. Then every element of the past, present and future is within this sphere. If this is true, then past, present and future already exist and are waiting to be discovered, invented or unveiled. This is a nonlinear coexistence of time differentials. If you were given a flashlight, the path you would light up is your life. The more light you shed, the more enlightened you become. As you continue to light more of this ball, you will become more adept at manipulating and relating to your environment until you can create the energy matrix that will, in turn, create the physical manifestations that you wish. The more evolved you become, the more frequencies you can interface with. The purpose of evolving is to light up the universe (which will enable you to be a co-creator and master the elements.) Then you can truly create. As you have peace within and around you, understand your latent potential. When you realize your relationship as a microcosm to the universal macrocosm—you have evolved to a higher plateau. It is necessary to study part by part, but then it is also necessary to recognize one's own place in relation to that of others. An over-emphasis on the individual self without the knowledge of the cosmic relationships only creates veils. To reiterate, free will is built into the system of evolved creatures for co-creation. There are possible paths; but once chosen, each path has its end result predetermined to fit in with the general matrix of the hologram.

EMOTIONS

There is no such thing as fear of the unknown as it is impossible to fear something for which there is no frame of reference. Fear drives us back to the past as it is those thoughts and patterns that are familiar. When you risk and stretch to new heights, fear dissipates due to a new comfort zone.

Feel what the energy of every emotion feels like when you are in the midst of happiness, depression, anxiety etc. Be aware of harmony and how to get back into that vibration when difficult situations occur. It involves being tuned into yourself and feeling the disturbances, but not adding to them and not denying them, but giving some space and time for things to settle again. Become aware of all the things you do which make it difficult to become centered. Then as each moment happens, you are absorbing it and not reacting to it or fighting it. If you become depressed, realize the vibration and go into deep breathing or relaxation to change the energy. Don't give names to experiences, but just feel the energy. When you don't know what is going on, you are forced to be with what is going on. Then shift into another vibration if you wish. When you practice shifting emotions and vibrations, you will get to the point that you don't have to practice anymore as you will just be what you want when you want. The shifting of energy will then be automatic.

When you are assessing a situation, look at the entire picture. You will readily see what is in alignment and what is not. For example, if you are looking at a person rocking back and forth in a room, it could become a terrible disturbance. When you are in balance, and then look at the entire room, the person rocking could then become a small motion rather than creating havoc in your field of vision.

EXERCISES

ENERGY FIELDS

 Take a partner, sit opposite and face him. Choose who is to be the sender and who is the receiver. Have the receiver close his eyes (just to block out any other stimuli), while the sender mentally sends an emotion directed to the receiver. This can be done by visualizing a symbol of the emotion. Peace may be sent as a dove or a heart. The emotion may be sent directly to the person's heart area or any other appropriate area. The receiver should talk about what he is feeling or sensing. These sensations are subtle. If you are not getting any response, change methods and try another symbol or send it to another part of the body. Try other emotions as well. The emotion of frustration will bring about a very different response and feeling. When you have done this several times, in various ways, change roles and now you become the receiver. Do this with many other partners so that you can experience various energies.

 This exercise is to prove to you that energy is real. The more you practice this, the easier it will become to sense whether someone is trying to deceive you or simply telling the truth. Successful people, in any endeavor, use their intuition and vibrations from others to gauge what they will or will not do. I had a corporate Board of Directors try this exercise. The president became elated when he started receiving various sensations because when he received the feeling of peace, it was the same feeling that he got when he would go along with a deal. When he sensed an uneasy feeling, it was the same feeling he got when he wouldn't touch the deal with a ten foot pole. Daily we unconsciously sense various aspects of situations. Be aware of what you are receiving and don't be fooled by the words. Connect with the energy output for your best decision.

GETTING RESULTS

Before you manage your energy to create something, know what it is you want. Get a mental picture of what you want to manifest. Once you choose your goal and set a cause into motion, direct your subconscious mind to think positively about the goal. Radiate out thoughts and pictures of that result. Know that anything unlike the energy radiating out is being pushed away while "like energy" is being attracted. As you radiate out, create vacuums. Clean out your thoughts and feelings, give up old images, create each day the way you want it to be and leave the past behind. Visualize that the goal has already happened. Know that positive thoughts plus faith, coupled with action, will start producing the desired results.

FEELING ENERGY

Sit comfortably and place your hands so that the palms face each other. Bring your palms about one-quarter of an inch apart.

Now separate the palms of your hands by about two inches and then slowly bring them back to the quarter of an inch. Then separate the palms by about four inches and slowly bring them back to their original position. Repeat this procedure and separate your palms by about six inches. Keep your motions slow and steady. As you return your hands to their original position, notice if you begin to feel a build-up of pressure between your hands. It may take the form of heat, tingling or feel like two north ends of a magnet slightly repelling each other. You may sense that you have an invisible soap bubble that can be stretched and slightly squooshed between your palms. Remember, these sensations are subtle. It may help you to close your eyes for deeper concentration.

Once again separate your palms to about eight inches apart. Do not immediately return your hands to their original position. Instead, as you bring your hands close together, experience the pressure field you have built up and sense how many sensations you feel.

These sensations validate the premise that you do not stop at your skin and that energy billows forth. You are feeling energy in various forms.

ENERGY SHIELD

In order to protect yourself from taking on another person's energy pattern, one must shield. Close your eyes and imagine yourself being put into a clear test tube that is about one foot taller than yourself and is open at the top. Program the energy that can come in by simply stating that only energy frequencies that are for your highest good can penetrate. Do this as you awake in the morning for protection. It can be repeated whenever you like to reinforce the shield.

SENSING ENERGY

Sit and stare at an object without blinking for about two minutes. Then close your eyes and take four deep breaths. Open your eyes again and continue staring at the space between you and the object that you were staring at. You will see sparkles or waves in the air. Then close your eyes again, take another few deep breaths, and quickly open your eyes. Staring into space again should produce these waves even more dramatically.

What you are seeing is the universal energy that is omnipresent and of which everything is composed. It is precisely these energy patterns that you utilize for healing and for manipulation. Energy just "is." You must decide how and what to do with it for your own purpose.

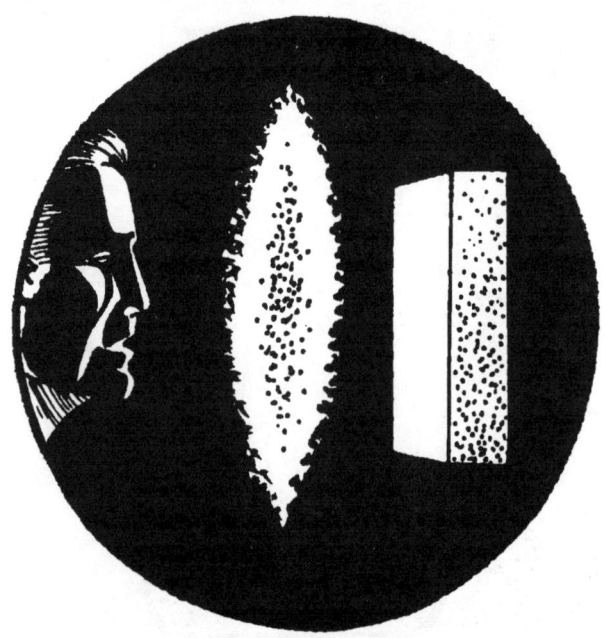

SENSING ENERGY FIELDS

There are energy points in the center of the palms of your hands. For the next two weeks reach for objects by out-stretching your palms toward the objects. As you near something, sense its energy field. Try shaking hands with a person by putting your hands out to each other, extend your left palm up and the other person extend his right palm down just inches above yours without making physical contact. Close your eyes and feel the energy between you. Move your hands up and down, closer and farther apart from each other's palm and experience the inner and outer limits of your energy fields.

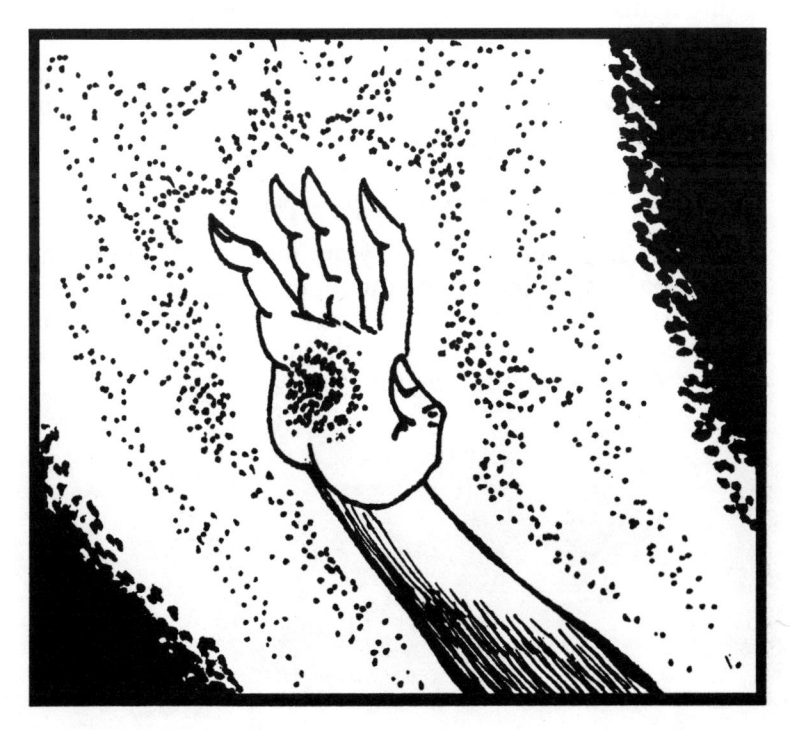

BREATH AND RELAXATION TECHNIQUES

Breathing is a constant source of energy and regeneration. When one changes a breathing pattern, thinking and feeling also changes. Slow breathing for five minutes can clear the mind for up to four hours and raises functioning to a higher level.

BASIC BREATHING

Inhale through your nose to a slow count of eight (the diaphragm goes out on the inhalation.) Hold the breath for four counts and then exhale through your nose to a count of eight (the diaphragm comes in on the exhalation.) Repeat this process six to twelve times. It will calm down all of your bodily processes and allow you to access your autonomic nervous system.

ABDOMINAL BREATHING

In this method you bring your diaphragm in on the inhalation and let the diaphragm out on the exhalation. This can blast mental blocks and pushes the breath to the upper portions of your body to oxygenate your organs and create quiet and calm while stilling the mind.

RELAXATION TECHNIQUES

Relaxation facilitates centering and balance. It encourages you to experience more of a connectedness with all things and the universe. Balance is flexibility, steadiness, stability and the ability to flow with unlimited possibilities.

RELAXATION USING LIGHT

Sit comfortably with your eyes closed. Imagine a white ball of light above your head. It is radiating energy and visualize it coming down and entering through the top of your head. As it comes down your body, imagine that it is purifying, balancing and energizing every muscle, tissue, organ, cell and pore that it touches. Picture this light cleansing and eliminating all impurities as it travels down your body and out the bottom of your feet.

GLASS BODY

Lie down, close your eyes and visualize your body being a transparent washing machine. Picture a liquid cleanser going throughout your body, taking with it anything that you want to rid yourself of and only leaving intact what is good for you. You can get rid of whatever emotions, physical ailments or stress that bother you. It will energize you to new heights and leave you feeling pure and clean with renewed clarity of thought.

SEEING THE ELECTRO-MAGNETIC FIELD

Look at the top of a tree and look to the right of it at the sky; look back at the tree and you will see a white glow around the tree which is its electro-magnetic field. If you are having difficulty detecting it, squint and stare six inches around the top of the tree and the glow will appear. The cells on the side of the eye can see faster than at the center so sometimes you may glimpse flashes or sparkles of light from objects and never realize that these flashes are the energy exuding from that object. Do this with a person. View a person in front of a white wall in dim light and the glow appears. Stare six inches above the person's head to see this light. The glow will appear as backlighting around the person's head. Colors can appear as well.

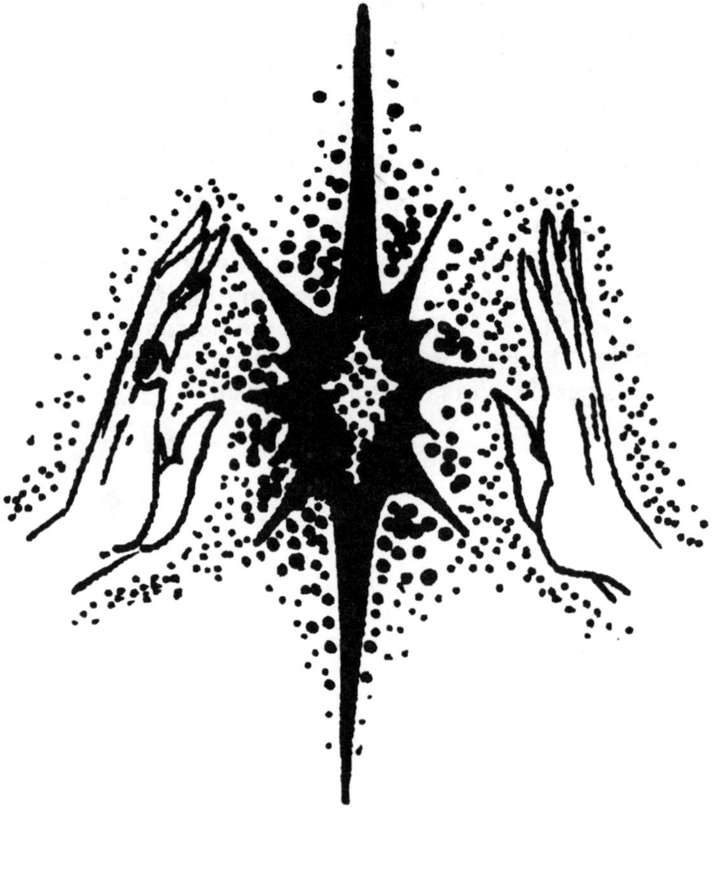

BREAKING THE STRESS BARRIER

GO FOR IT!

   According to the Random House Dictionary, the definition of stress is: any stimulus, as fear or pain, that disturbs or interferes with the normal physiological equilibrium of an organism. Therefore, stress is the rate of wear and tear within the body. Stress disorders are based upon the slow, developmental accumulation of psychological and physical stress responses throughout the life of the individual. That simply means that it is not the stress itself that creates our problems, but how we perceive and cope with it. What I may consider stress may be joy for you. I love lecturing and speaking in front of people; this could be your nightmare. That which is a struggle to one person is a gentle effort to another. Stress is always HOW you feel about something—your opinion. When your emotion is negative, find out about your underlying opinion and slightly change the way in which you view it to rid yourself of this negative feeling. We think faster than we act; so things generally take longer to happen than we expect. Always look at your options, then look for the angles you may have missed. Collect all the facts before you "go for it."

❁ ❁ ❁

STRESSORS

Stress is a state that one is in, and not an agent that produces such a state. The agent or stimulus that elicits the stress reaction is called a stressor. We react to these stressors with various intensities. There are minor stressors on one end and major stressors on the other. Most of what is encountered daily are minor stressors such as getting up late, choosing what to wear, or what to eat. They are usually handled easily. More intense factors such as death, divorce or loss of a job can be major stressors. All stressors, minor or major, elicit the stress response to some degree and require that we adapt or cope to stay balanced. If you can learn to manage each situation with respect to your own priorities, rather than to those that are being thrust upon you, you will be in control of the situation.

Illness can happen when clusters of major events occur within a short period of time. A major step toward establishing a true preventative medicine would occur if destructive, dysfunctional, high-stress behavior can be recognized early and changed. Rising above the frustration, stress, and anxiety of conflict can only be mastered by controlling the inner states of thought. These thoughts can be brought under control by meditative and relaxation techniques.

There are special events throughout life that are intense stressors. They are specific to developmental stages of growth. Going to school for the first time is one of those events. Graduating, marriage, having children, starting a new job, retirement, and divorce are just a few others. These can be viewed either as positive or negative. Each requires adaptation and flexibility for change. It is when a number of major life changes happen in a short period of time that the person has a harder time coping and the stress level intensifies. These can serve as a predictor of illness, injury or psychological problems if these stressors are not handled properly.

STRESS SYNDROME

Stress is a necessary part of life and it can be a great motivator. "Eustress" is a term used to designate desirable stress. It is the stress that is experienced to maintain life, such as through cardiovascular regulation, digestion, and hormonal secretions. Desirable stress also includes events in which you are challenged and perceive the potential for personal growth. How one perceives a stressor is a prime determinant of eustress. A performer or athlete uses stress to "get up for performing." During the performance, controlled and directed stress helps bring out their best. However, when we are not successfully channeling the stress in our lives, our body's reaction becomes negative and goes into a phase called "Fight or Flight Syndrome." During this phase of DISTRESS, certain physiological changes begin to take place: the heart begins to beat faster from adrenaline being released into the system, blood is channeled into the large muscles of the body, and the functions of the immune and digestive systems are inhibited. Should distress continue over time, body organs and systems can become fatigued. This wear and tear can result in illness or dysfunction.

After a period of time, if the stress is not counteracted, the person experiences the DIS-EASE PHASE, sometimes related to frustration—the inability to change an aggravating situation. Due to a suppressed immune and digestive system, the normal functioning of the body is out of balance. We sometimes say, "We are run-down and have caught a bug." In essence we are describing a person who has been in the DIS-EASE PHASE of stress too long. Research has shown that a person experiencing a prolonged period of DIS-EASE has a higher portion of the stress syndrome than a person who was taking some precautions or actions to address the stress in his life. *Stress can control us or we can learn to control it.* Learning to control stress, not avoiding it, is the challenge. Controlling stress encourages us to view life in a positive manner. It is learning how to become more congruent with the challenge that makes your life work better.

MANAGING STRESS

There are three important steps to managing stress. First, assess your signs and symptoms of the stress response, the sources of stress, and appropriate stress-management techniques. Second, intervene to prevent or reduce the stress response. Third, establish a social support group that will reinforce your attempts to manage stress. The goal of stress management is to channel stress to promote stimulation and growth.

Some people worry so much about attaining their goal that they miss the beauty of the experiences. They only feel stress and tension until the goal has become accomplished. Use this as an analogous example: There are two apple seeds. One apple thinks that it must become a strong tree and does. The other never thought about growing, but wanted it's apples to be red or yellow, juicy or tart, bearing much fruit, while still trying to create roots. This seed has wasted energy on thinking what would happen after it grew. Where do you fit in and do you cause yourself unnecessary anxiety?

For you to grow from where you are now and to live every day to its fullest, you must have some idea of what you want to do or become. Goals are never really meant to be accomplished; but to give you direction. If you only had the one goal in mind, you could be unaware of other better opportunities that come along. Being flexible allows these other approaches and ideas to filter into your consciousness as well. These can lead to different paths and other goals that may be even better for you. Anything outstanding that you accomplish with your life must be done with the help of other people. This network becomes a working aid and a support group for you. Brainstorming with others compounds ideas and solutions. To demonstrate this I gave each person in my seminar a conch shell and told them that they had five minutes to list all of the uses for it. When they each had their list, I then had them pair off with another person and gave them three minutes to compare their lists. Instead of just coming up with two separate lists, they were able to quadruple what they had as one idea led to another. That is why team work is great. Ideas multiply and feed off one another. If you are to enlarge your dimensions of life, you must learn to listen to others deeply, eagerly, and openly. Too many times we don't really listen to another point of view.

POSITIVE THOUGHTS

Conflicts are only conditions about which no decisions have been made. Your state of consciousness now will be your state of being of the future. Life is an extension of thought. What you hold in your mind today, you will soon experience. Everything starts out as a thought. A building was only a thought in an architect's mind, the painting was a thought to the painter, the dress a thought to the designer, and you become what you think you are. Every few minutes most of us have an unkind thought about ourselves: "It was dumb of me to have done that." "I'm so stupid to have let that happen." "What a klutz I am." And the list goes on. If you multiply these thoughts times 24 hours a day, times 365 days a year, times how old you are in years, look at what you are reinforcing. You should be giving yourself credit for the times that you show up when you are supposed to, for the good work that you have accomplished, for cleaning the house, for going grocery shopping, even for smiling at someone else to make them happy. When we reinforce these things, we feel better about ourselves. Just about any problem that comes up can be handled, if we have a feeling of self-worth. A belief, held tenaciously in the mind for a period of time, will absolutely and undeniably be fulfilled in your life. Therefore, make sure that your beliefs are what you want, as a self-fulfilling prophecy is in the making at every given moment. It takes 97 muscles to frown and 18 to smile. Which seems to make more sense to you?

Once an individual is held in place, either dedicated by choice or necessity to face every problem, to deal with all challenges, to handle the highs and lows of each day—then growth is inevitable.

If something works in your life, hang on to it. If something doesn't work, let it go. Take inventory periodically. Because something worked for you in the past, doesn't mean that it still has value in the present.

To believe in yourself, find a talent, skill, ability, or parcel of knowledge with which you can excel. Then pursue it. You are responsible for the ways that others treat you. You act; people react. People get so busy with the results of success that they stop doing the things that made them successful.

Too often we are looking back to the past or looking forward to the future and pay very little attention to what is going on in the present. Life is now. Now is the future you were looking forward to yesterday. This moment in time is when the infinite future and the past meet. What you do, think, and act now is creating the future you want tomorrow. They are all contributing factors to the future and they are all happening in the present.

There is a branch of science known as psycho-neuro-immunology. It advocates that attitudes affect the nervous system and, in turn, affect the immune system. The adverse effects of stress can manifest themselves as ulcers, changes in blood sugar, hypertension and headaches. It is purported that 85% of all illnesses are psycho-induced or stress-related. Endured over a period of time, the hoarded pressure of stress must find a release. Therefore, it is important to become aware of what beliefs and attitudes you have and how it is affecting your health. Flexibility is an important factor as it is the ability to see the problems of the present as learning experiences and to turn what might have been destructive pressures into the means of achieving higher levels of integration.

PHYSICAL REACTIONS

Some physical reactions to stress are: dilated pupils, heartbeat speeding up, increased blood pressure, digestion slowing down, increased pulse rate, hormones entering the blood to increase coagulating ability, endocrine glands releasing hormones—including adrenaline—an increased rate of breathing, and changes in the galvanic skin response. Due to chronic muscle tensions the function of the immune system is inhibited, and the oxygen-rich blood is diverted away from the skin to the brain and skeletal muscles.

Much of the therapeutic research is based on the assumption that disease is caused by bacteria. This has produced a continuous wave of new products and new medicines at considerable cost in time, effort, health and money. Many people argue that orthodox medicine has impressively reduced the death rate all over the world, but if we look around us, we can see that the incidences of mental and emotional illness have increased proportionately. What holistic practitioners do is to reduce the patient's susceptibility by bringing the person into a balanced state where it is impossible for bacteria to survive.

HOLISTIC VS. TRADITIONAL

The term holistic simply means that the whole entity has an existence other than the sum of its parts.

The traditional way to treat disease differs from the holistic practitioner in various ways.

HOLISTIC PRACTITIONER
1. Treats the patient's causes as well as the symptoms.
2. Treats the physical, mental and emotional aspects.
3. Believes that each individual is unique.
4. Practitioner regards health as the ratio that the individual is functioning to his optimum capacity to function.
5. Patients are treated constructively with nutrition, awareness, exercise and care.
6. Advocates that disease comes from disharmony in the mental, emotional and physical aspects of the person.
7. Practitioner promotes patient self-responsibility.

TRADITIONAL PRACTITIONER
1. Treats only the symptoms of the disease.
2. Patients are treated only as physical beings.
3. Treats patients metabolically alike.
4. Regards health as the absence of disease.
5. Treats disease destructively: surgery, drugs, radiation.
6. Disease comes from germs.
7. Patient should self-surrender to the doctor.

The holistic point of view states that health is a state of complete physical, mental and social well-being, and not merely an absence of disease. The individual's wellness is a process that constructs a self-designed style of living that allows the person to live life to the fullest. Most people do not function at their full potential and only maintain life; whereas fully functioning people enhance life. To begin a wellness life-style, first make a commitment to yourself: assess your current life-style; and take action—investigate information, locate resources for skill development, and build a support network. These are some of the steps to fulfill for self-actualization—a drive to achieve your full potential, to be all that you can possibly be. It is the need to stretch, risk and grow.

SYMPTOMS OF STRESS

A connection exists between the mental, physical, and emotional aspects of a person. If there is a problem mentally, it will affect the emotional, and probably appear as a symptom in the physical body. If a person is having a physical problem, it will also affect the mental and emotional aspects. When you consider the problem to be minor, you can have a simple stress response which may take the form of a head, throat or stomach ache. After the response, the person goes back to functioning in a normal manner. When the stress is prolonged, ambiguous, undefined or can't be changed (your children are misbehaving, mother is living with you, the relationship is not working, your job is awful), the normal stress response no longer works and the immune system tends to be suppressed for the reasons listed in the paragraph of "physical reactions to stress." Other illnesses can manifest themselves because our line of defense, the immune system, is not working properly. Stress can create an acidosis condition in our body resulting in tooth decay, gall stones or kidney stones. Stress-induced disorders can include cardiovascular conditions, cancer, arthritis, and respiratory diseases. Think of the times that you were stressed and how you responded mentally, emotionally and physically. A common response to stress is to ignore its effect on the mind and body, and to seek respite in alcohol, tranquilizers and other medications—but these are not solutions.

Health exists when you are balanced mentally, emotionally and physically. Illness results when stress and conflict disrupt this process. For example, if a person is confronted with a stressful situation that he finds overwhelming, he makes an unconscious choice which allows him a means of coping with this situation. One resolution is to develop a psychosomatic disorder, such as a headache, which affects him to the point of being incapacitated and releases him from the responsibilities which are bothering him. These symptoms free him from dealing with the situation; his family and peers diminish their demands upon him, and he receives tender loving care. Once this course of action proves successful, there is a tendency on the part of the person to reinitiate this same pattern of behavior response to future stressors. The response of the headache is usually made at an unconscious level. This must be brought to consciousness so the person can become aware of this behavior pattern. Stress affects an individual through his autonomic responses. Practicing relaxation techniques is a great preventor of psychosomatic disease. The body has two conditions: relaxed or tense. If you can keep the body calm and centered, headaches could be controlled or relieved: blood pressure can be lowered; brain waves slowed down; plus the heart and pulse rate can be lowered. Millions of people are taking Valium or Librium and continue on drug maintenance for the alleviation of nervous tension, only to spend their lives in a state of sedation. An important accomplishment of the meditative therapies is that they teach people to exercise control over their autonomic functions. These functions include brain waves, heart rate, and muscle tension. One of the most important features of the holistic system of healing is the change in the person's belief system in adopting the concept that he is an active and responsible participant in the process of self-healing and not a passive victim of disease. The progression toward disease can be interrupted through the use of stress-reduction techniques. Exercises for these are at the end of the chapter.

BENEFITS OF RELAXATION TECHNIQUES

1. They are enjoyable;
2. They can decrease symptoms of illness such as headache, nausea, and diarrhea;
3. They can increase levels of physical energy;
4. They can increase concentration;
5. They can increase efficiency;
6. They can increase feelings of self-confidence;
7. They are helpful in the treatment of insomnia;
8. They can lower blood pressure;
9. They can lower emotional arousal so that the body stays in a state of homeostasis and balance.

REACTION TO STRESS

The way we react to stress is more important than the stress itself. To some people a roller coaster ride is a torture chamber, and to others it is a thrill. They are all having the same experience, but they are reacting to it differently. Every problem we encounter in life can be viewed positively or negatively. Changing the way you think—viewing a difficult assignment at work as a chance to improve your skills, for example—can change a life of stress to a life of challenge and excitement. Stresses that we choose evoke a totally different response from those we'd like to avoid. Every person's stress level varies. If the stress is considered to be minor, we can generally handle it well and get on with our lives. If too many adversities come at once, we may not be as efficient. If it is a stressor that we have been avoiding, the coping becomes even more difficult. Whenever we choose a situation, even if it entails some stressful factors, we have time to figure out how to handle it and tend to cope much better than if it is put upon us.

Being balanced is easy when everything is going our way; but it is more difficult to be poised when things seem to be going wrong. Being centered goes "off-balance" quickly when the refrigerator goes on the blink, we trip and fall, the car doesn't start, and our head starts to pound. Relaxation exercises help to keep the mind and body calm so that we think and react in a more cohesive manner. We have all experienced times when we feel great: someone may say a rude remark and we still don't react negatively. However, if things have not been going so well or we are not feeling so wonderful, that same remark can create tension and our response will be quite different. Therefore, the same comment creates a totally different response only because of the way we are feeling at that moment. Words are merely words until we put meaning to them. In one of my classes I told this woman that she looked beautiful. She started to cry which was totally inappropriate for my compliment until she explained that this was the dress she was wearing when her boyfriend broke up with her. My words were a trigger for her to associate the outfit with a situation that she has still not resolved.

Many times you may get stressed out over what is really someone else's problem—the salesperson that is using you as a scapegoat, the friend that is having a bad day and lacing into you, and the mother that is talking, "only for your own good." I'm sure you can think of a million other examples of how you have allowed other people's problems to become your own. How often has a situation occurred where you wished that you had said, done, or reacted differently and then verbally beat yourself up because you hadn't?

SOUNDING BOARD

Everyone needs a sounding board at times. It's easier for someone else to give you an objective opinion because they are not emotionally involved in the situation. One way to be your own sounding board is to view the situation that has made you upset. In order to do this, close your eyes and visualize a movie screen in front of you. Mentally view this entire situation on the screen. Review every detail. Don't be judgmental; just play it through like you would a regular movie, even though one of the characters just happens to look like you. When you finish your story; open your eyes. You will generally find that it is not as emotionally upsetting as you thought. The difference is that when you view the situation in front of you, it allows you to detach emotionally. Then it doesn't have the same kind of power over you. This exercise shows you where it may have been your fault, someone else's, or anything in between. It also is a tool for helping you handle this type of situation in the future. If you are still emotionally attached after viewing it, do it again. Each time you see it, you will detach more and more until you will be so tired of this same boring story that you will just let it go and not bother with it anymore.

This same exercise is great for viewing future events. For example, if you are going on an interview, visualize the entire process and every conceivable outcome. You may picture yourself getting the job, not getting it, and every other possible answer. What this movie screen allows you to do is to pick yourself up and go back to functioning normally in a shorter period of time. If you were thinking positively and didn't get the job, you might be devastated. By using this process, even not getting the job won't put you into an extreme low since you have already experienced that as one of your outcomes. You won't be thrilled, but you can be in control, and use the opportunity to start again with strength instead of self pity.

There are very few situations worth getting that upset about. We don't function well when we are off-center and tend to act from our emotions rather than being rational. One of my students called me up a couple of months after she learned the movie screen exercise and related the following story: Her husband had been traveling for two weeks, came home and started yelling at her through the bathroom door about her irresponsibility for not having toilet paper there. She almost started to yell back and tell him to get it himself. When she visualized the scene, she just started to laugh instead. Here she had not seen her husband in two weeks, missed him and would be not speaking to him for the rest of the night because of toilet paper. Instead, she just got it, apologized, and all turned out well. She claims that the evening would have been a cold war if she had not put up the visualization screen.

Use this technique any time you want to disassociate from a situation. It will nip many arguments in the bud, allow you to see more rationally, and help you to balance yourself quicker.

TIPS TO EASE TENSION

1. Think about something else. Shifting your perspective distracts you and breaks whatever chain of thought that is producing the stress.

2. Think positively. Thinking about a success or past achievement puts you into a positive and confident state of mind to act with ease.

3. Take a mental vacation. Visualize a place where you want to be and are happy. It will relax you immediately.

4. Get up and leave. Leaving the scene or changing position can help relax you and create a different posture for clearer and more relaxed behavior.

5. Take several deep breaths. Deep breathing relaxes and slows down the autonomic nervous system resulting in calmness.

6. Stretch. Relaxing tight muscles and even massaging them eases tension.

7. Take a warm bath or just run warm water over your hands until you feel the tension drain away.

8. Exercise. Even taking a walk around the block can help alleviate tension.

9. Listen to a relaxation tape.

10. Listen to music that relaxes you.

WHAT DO YOU REALLY WANT?

It is more important to question the underlying patterns of personal dissatisfaction and to discover what is limiting achievement than to look for answers to specific problems. How does what we learn influence the way we think and work, the quality of our lives and our definitions of success and happiness? Education may help us make better choices for our lives, but only coupled with experience can we develop enough wisdom to stabilize our lives and perhaps recognize some paths for satisfaction. Many times we repeat old patterns hoping for different results, but without a new approach, the outcome will be the same as the past. With the growth of better insights, we can learn more quickly through our experiences and convert what we learn into new knowledge that we can apply. We may be trying to take care of ourselves without knowing our real needs. We keep feeding ourselves what we think we need only to find ourselves growing more desperate and more dissatisfied. How can we maintain that inner peace, balance and strength through our daily events and emotional upheavals? Changing our outer circumstances—jobs, relationships or environment may help temporarily. We must uncover repeating patterns that rob us of time and energy. We must look closely at what we are doing and evaluate if these actions are likely to bring us the satisfaction we need. When we can objectively see limiting views and attitudes, then we can counter avoidance and self-deception and then establish clearer priorities for our lives.

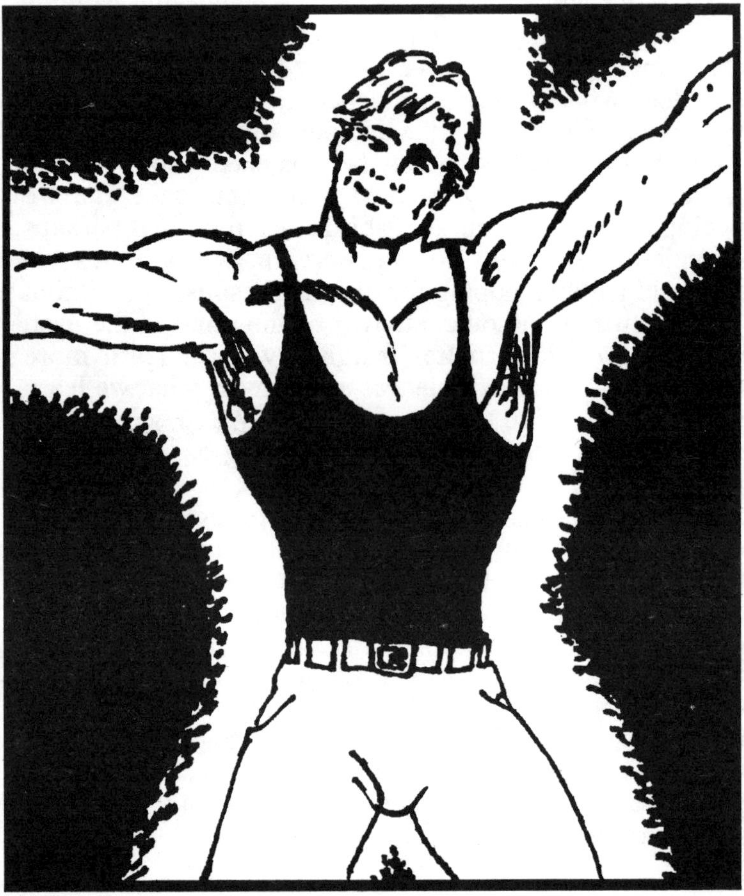

EXERCISES

RESISTANCE

Most people feel uncomfortable with change. When a person joins a class, she usually takes the same seat for every session, stays with the same job even though it is no longer fulfilling, maintains the same relationship as another may be worse, and gravitates to the same restaurants instead of trying new ones. Even though many of these self-created situations could now be considered stressful, we find that we still resist change. If any of these seem familiar, reevaluate your logic to see why you procrastinate.

COMMON REASONS FOR RESISTANCE

I. We can use the Logic of Assumption.
  1. It wouldn't do any good anyway.
  2. He won't understand.
  3. I would have to change my personality to fit in.
  4. They can't give me what I need.

Then there is resistance due to Limiting Ideas.
  1. It's just not done.
  2. It's not right.
  3. It's too far.
  4. I'm too short.

II. Sometimes we give our power away and use that as resistance to change.
  1. This isn't the right environment.
  2. My doctor won't allow me.
  3. I can't get the time off.
  4. They say I'm too young (too fat, too serious, too weak.)

III. There are the Delaying Tactics.
  1. I'll do it later.
  2. It doesn't seem like the right time for it.
  3. I can't think right now.
  4. I'm too busy and don't have the time it takes.

This one should hit a familiar note—Denial.
 1. I can't do anything about this problem.
 2. What good would it do to change?
 3. If I ignore it, it will go away.

IV. This is one of the biggest reasons—Fear.
 1. I'm not ready yet.
 2. I might fail.
 3. They might reject me.
 4. I don't know enough.
 5. I might get hurt.
 6. It might cost me money.
 7. I'm afraid to express my feelings.

At some point in our lives we all hesitate, procrastinate and are not extremely comfortable with change. One thing to remember is that you know what you have, and if you are not happy with it, realize that you will only get more of the same by staying in the situation.

List all of the things that you would like changed in your life. Then prioritize the list and try to change the one that is causing you the most stress and difficulty. If you cannot extricate yourself from it immediately, list the choices you have that will create options for you to cope better. Knowing what it is that you want changed and the choices for handling it in a more positive fashion will start you in a new direction and make you feel more powerful and in control.

AFFIRMING CHANGE

Many times we try to relax one part of our body only to find that some other part has tightened up. It's like a good news/bad news story. We must learn to recognize what happens to us in various situations. Notice what your body and mind feel like when they are relaxed, and what parts change when tension occurs.

Look in the mirror and say, "I am willing to change." Take note what happens to your body. Breathe deeply and repeat the statement six times and do a token gesture to make that change. Then notice how much easier it is to talk about change and feel more comfortable with the idea. First comes awareness and then the action. The initial step for change is always the hardest, but it gets easier every step of the way.

As you are looking at yourself in the mirror, another statement to make is, "I deserve to have ____." Then think of all the reasons you want it and why you deserve it. When you have the confidence that you deserve it, change becomes a simpler task.

Too many times the mirror is used for criticizing what you see. Now you are utilizing it for positive statements that can benefit you.

★ ★ ★

POSITIVE FUTURES

Too often we protect things that we can touch and do nothing about protecting ourselves. Pressure builds up as we worry about our income; think about how the most money could be made with the least amount of effort; how unhappy we may be in our relationship; ponder as to why we are more tired after sleep; and feel miserable knowing that tomorrow's routine will be the same as today's. By adding some of these stressors together, we find that we clog up and that we can no longer work efficiently or think clearly. This exercise allows a transmutation of feelings which results in new perspectives. The pressure becomes diffused as you transmute these feelings into something more positive.

Close your eyes and picture a movie screen in front of you. Visualize all the events of the day. If any negative aspects show up, stop the movie and see how this negative portion could be transformed into positives. By doing this you are, in essence, neutralizing what has disturbed you. The reward is that your feelings will now be acting positively on negative acts of past events. Do not think in terms of right or wrong, but of negatives and positives. A more positive future can only come from a more positive view of the past.

CONFIDENCE

Sometimes confusion is positive as it can promote change. When we are hesitating and not changing, we can find ourselves settling for things which may not be in our best interest. One way to find out what we really want is to write down this statement: "If I knew I'd make a difference, something I'd be doing that I'm not doing now is ___." Then see if it is worth putting the effort into your life to access this desire.

✧ ✧ ✧

STRESSORS

Make an integrity list. That is, list the major areas of your life: such as your job, personal life, relationships, home, health, recreation, etc. Review this list and put subtopics under these main headings. For example, under the topic of relationship could be: parents, children, boyfriend, friends, boss, or peers. On a scale of 1-10, rate how you feel that you are coping with each topic. When there is a low rating, figure out why it is not up to your liking, what could be done about it, and re-commit to making it better. Listing these topics can make it obvious as to the sections that need more attention.

ACCENTUATE THE POSITIVE

The easiest way to actually see what you consider your strengths and what you consider to be your weaknesses is to draw three columns on a piece of paper. Label the first column STRENGTHS and list all of yours in this section. The second column is labeled WEAKNESSES and contains what you consider your weaknesses (what you don't feel you do well or just don't like to do even though you have to.) Label the third column CHANGE and list how you can move the items from column two into column one.

You do not have to reinvent the wheel to transmute your efforts into positive ones. For instance, if you like to travel yet you don't like to spend time in the car, your method of coping better could be listening to audio tapes of music or lectures so that the time passes quickly. Another example is that you may love your job, but dislike your office space. Transforming it with pictures, flowers, or your own personal touch could change this environment into someplace pleasurable. A third example could be that you know that exercise is good for you, but you don't like to do it. The method for change may be to incorporate it into your regular routine—stretches while ironing; squats while putting things away; or lunges while vacuuming or sweeping. Make sure that you go to a personal trainer who will show you the correct way of doing these motions. Then you will get the most benefit from it and not get hurt from doing improper movements. A creative idea can make the most unpleasant task pleasurable.

STRESS REDUCERS

It is easy to feel undue pressure when certain words are anchored. The term "should" is a cause for frustration. Try using the term "can" instead and feel how the pressure has eased.

You can be more objective about your feelings by simply changing a simple statement. For example, don't say, "I am angry." Say, "I am feeling angry." This allows you to switch to *feeling* another emotion if you so desire.

When visualizing, don't use negatives as the unconscious will relate to the CAN'T, DON'T etc. If you want to lose weight, state that you are filled and satisfied with a smaller portion. Not "I am heavy and want to lose weight" as the unconscious relates to *heavy* and *weight*. Say, "I am satisfied with healthy food that will benefit me."

To have a better memory, state "I am improving my memory everyday" rather than "I have a poor memory that I want to improve."

To stop smoking: picture and state that "I am relaxed and aware of the substances that I am putting into my body that will help me." This is more positive than saying "I want to quit smoking." In this last statement the mind relates to the word *smoking*.

Make sure that your visualizations and affirmations are all positive. Pick out the most negative statement about yourself and change it to a positive statement. Use this statement for one month and notice changes within you.

SCHEDULE

Sometimes there is not enough play in our lives as work takes precedence. In order to insure a balance of both work and play, use a red pen to mark your calendar with all work related activities. Mark the calendar in blue with your play time. Glancing at this will clearly point out whether you have balanced your day, week or month. If not, rearrange it so that you have plenty of time for both.

FROM BURNOUT TO SUCCESS

HEALTH AND BALANCE

Before you can create order, you must undo burnout. Your outer world is a reflection of your inner one. Your desk, house, body, job and relationships are as good as the inner workings of the self. When this is in order, you will have the energy, stamina and enthusiasm to get the best out of life.

Look on the bright side of your current situation. Having more things to do than you think you could ever accomplish means you are alive, growing and thriving.

The first thing to do is to get your body in good working order. Reestablish healthful eating and exercise habits. Consume foods that are low in fat, salt and sugar, and high in complex carbohydrates: fruits, vegetables, whole grains, pasta, potatoes—and plenty of water. If you can, exercise for at least 30 minutes 3 times a week. Take a relaxing walk. Fatigue is a result of acidic buildup of lactic acid in your body as well as dehydration and the breakdown of body tissue. You are overdoing it if you're very tired and your legs feel heavy. Don't exercise when you are sick. When your body is fighting exhaustion and infection, exercise is not what it needs.

To get to the balance that you want in life, take a step back from your life and view it objectively. How important are those "gottas" and "have to's?" Make a list of what you would do if you had six months to live in perfect health. Take a close look at the list because it represents the things in life that you presently value the most. This will put your life into perspective as to how you are living and how you really wish to live. Are they congruent? If not, what do you have to add or eliminate to make it a reality?

The next step is gaining proportion in your life. A true sign of burnout is exaggerating your dilemmas. Shrink things back to normal size. List the major problems in your life (you are ten pounds overweight, relationship problems, mortgage payments, etc.) Envision the very worst that could result from these problems. Can you live with it? If so, accept the situation and try to modify it the best you can. Write down some steps you can take to correct it. If the situation is intolerable, devise a strategy to make it acceptable even if it means finding another course of action.

Next, list your priorities. Decide which goals need attention now, and which ones can wait. Look at your interests, skills and needs, as well as what you are trying to do with your life. These will also be deciding factors to concentrate on as these are the priorities that will help you reach your goals faster.

For balance, you need to divide your life into three categories: career, relationships and personal growth. A fair share should be given to all three areas. To make sure this happens, keep a calendar of events and mark all personal events in red and mark career events in blue. A quick look at the calendar will show you if balance prevails. Take a mental inventory of your friends and put your energy into the people who are growing with you. Otherwise you will feel an energy drain.

Stress and crisis are in everyone's life, however when you are in balance, you don't lose your perspective. It's easy to keep things in proportion and prioritizing is a natural process. You are more likely to be sociable and to use your right brain creativity to solve problems. When you have high self-esteem, you have a can-do attitude even if your schedule is booked. Nothing seems overwhelming. Go one step and one day at a time; focus on the NOW. With these strategies, balance becomes a way of life.

BURNOUT

Stress and burnout are the building blocks of imbalance; they build slowly until you are left with the symptoms of stress that you can no longer ignore: muscle tension, aching back, headache, gastro-intestinal problems, colds and allergies, skin rash, hair loss, acne, and so on. Many different factors from how we eat to how we exercise can contribute to burnout. Here are a few culprits:

1. Junk food diets: The high salt and sugar content of junk food makes us even more anxious and irritable and puts us at a higher risk for heart disease.

2. Exercise abuse: Over-exercising is damaging to health. Make sure an exercise physiologist or trainer gives you a proper program that benefits your needs.

3. Bad posture: Since our spines must be vertical for fresh oxygen to come in and carbon dioxide to go out, working slumped over a desk for hours builds up more stress as we use only a third of our lung capacity in this position. Carbon dioxide gets trapped inside on every exhalation so we can feel exhausted, lightheaded and nauseated.

4. Sleep deprivation: The only time our cells totally regenerate are when we sleep. When you don't get enough sleep, it's physically and emotionally stressful.

5. Fluorescent lights: Working under such lights depletes our entire store of vitamin C, potassium and magnesium. Most corporations have noticed this and have changed to all-spectrum lighting.

6. Air conditioning and heat: Both dehydrate us. We may breathe the same stale air along with recirculated impurities such as fumes from the copy machine or someone else's smoke. This can cause us to keep sneezing for days.

7. Noise pollution: Noise from printers, telephones, refrigerators, T.V.s, and even office chatter can fray our nervous system.

8. Now or never: Because we live in a world that expects it *now*, we often make well-intentioned dysfunctional choices to ease the stress. Get back into balance and the choices become naturally easier to decipher.

STRATEGIES FOR ACCESSING MOOD CHANGES

1. Look at the funny side of a serious situation. By making light of a heavy predicament, you immediately de-escalate it. Blow it totally out of proportion until it becomes absurd and funny. Before you get aggravated when you are stuck in a traffic jam, think of yourself still there until you are old and gray. Even the prospect of that makes the scene ridiculous and will calm you.

2. Look for the positive aspects instead of the negatives. Use your adrenaline to pick yourself up and move forward.

3. Use your right brain creativity for problem solving. Put yourself in learning situations. Become the student instead of the teacher.

4. Pursue a goal. Reestablish your dreams and work toward them.

5. Nurture yourself by taking time out to play. Working for hours at a time tires the mind. Take some time out for fun. It will clear your mind and make your body feel better. Then go back to work with renewed vigor.

6. Try relaxation techniques, guided imagery or yoga.

Any combination of these strategies will allow you to extricate yourself from the situation to gain new insights and different perspectives. In doing so, the problems will not seem so monumental and can be handled easier and with less emotionality. These techniques can help bring you back to balance.

STEPS FOR SUCCESS

There are winning behaviors you need to master for success either in business or in your personal life.

In order to reach your true potential you must have an all-consuming passion. If the passion is not there, it is easy to give up when the project becomes difficult. It is only that passion that keeps you going even when the going gets tough.

You must have the belief of who you are, what you can become and realize that whatever your mind can conceive, your mind can achieve. Know that your mind is the most complex computer and that you have no limitations.

You must incorporate a strategy of organizing resources to work to your potential. Seek out other people who have accomplished similar goals. Their success may be in totally different areas, but their strategy may be adaptable and can be utilized to suit your needs.

Making your values clear and knowing what matters in your life will make it easier to manifest what you want. If your goals are not clear, sift out what you don't want and see what is left. The more specific you are about what you do want makes the goal easier to accomplish.

You must have the energy and vibrancy for success. Make sure you are not just achieving an isolated incident to be accomplished, but that you are designing a life that you want.

You must have the ability to develop a deep rapport with others. This is great not only to use for networking, but to have as a resource and as a support group.

In order to produce new results you must have mastery of communication both from within and without. Goals are only signposts pointing you in a certain direction. Thoughts have no power over us unless we give in to them. Thoughts are only words strung together. They have no meaning whatsoever until we choose what sort of meaning to give them. Choose to think thoughts that nourish and support you.

Try this exercise: Monitor your thoughts for one hour and notice the words you think about yourself. It is said that we think one negative or hurtful remark about ourselves every few minutes. Multiply these negative thoughts times the hours in a day, the days in a year, and times your age to see how many repetitions of these negatives are reinforced in your life. Starting now—become aware of those thoughts and start reinforcing the positive.

STRATEGY FOR SUCCESS

The first step for reaching success is to ask for what you want. Many people go through life assuming that others know what they want. Ask precisely and specifically, but ask. Even in your personal life don't assume that your partner knows you want to go to the movies and that he is reading the newspaper for spite. He may think that you are as content as he is. Say what you want and don't assume.

Ask someone who has the ability to help you. Too often we ask a person who is not in a position to help and we take that as a rejection when we are refused.

Make sure that person's needs are filled first and that value is created for the other person. If this is done, it becomes easier for the other person to want to help you.

Keep changing approaches until you get what you want. Learn from your rejections and don't get despondent. Don't give up; just try another way.

The more you celebrate success, the more a success consciousness is built. Too often we pass little goals by without acknowledgment and harp on what didn't happen. Celebrate all the little successes to build up self-esteem.

Try this exercise: If it would be impossible to fail, what would you do right now in your life? What activities and actions would you do (and be specific)? This can point you in the direction that you really need to succeed, so take note and have fun in the process.

Another way to realize what you want is to finish this sentence five different ways. "I should _____." Then ask, "why?" Now reread your sentences by saying, "If I really wanted to, I could _____." This changes the meaning completely. Now ask yourself, "Why haven't I?"

These techniques may show what you really want, the resistance you have in accomplishing it, and what it may take to motivate yourself into just doing it. The process must be fun or the results never seem worth it.

LADDER OF SUCCESS

Wrong-doing is only the result of wrong-thinking. By changing your thinking, the results will change; therefore, the proper thinking will produce the results you want. Review even what you consider the wrong results and find out what you can learn from them. There are no such things as failures—only results.

People who fear failure develop a fear of what might not work in advance. Then they feel it is pointless to take action as they are not going to succeed anyway. They sabotage their own success and never develop a success mentality. Know the purpose that you have, and the clarity of how to do it will become more apparent. Losers always have excuses as to why they failed and never seem to learn from the experience. Therefore, success is not in their future until they take responsibility for the good and the bad, and learn from both.

Semantics are important. If you feel work is hard, it will be. If you regard work as play, you will relax more, let your guard down, and become much more creative. Again, the process of work must be fun or you will never feel that the results are worth it.

Commitment is essential for success. Interest fades after a period of time. A person who is more committed will surpass a person who has more talent but is not as committed.

As a success technique look in the mirror. Since language is 90% non-verbal and 10% verbal, body language is very important. Other people's opinions of you are formed in the first 20 seconds after seeing you. Analyze yourself in the mirror. Are you standing up straight? Is your posture good? Do you look people straight in the eyes? What do you notice that evokes strength and character? If you met this person that you are looking at in the mirror, would you trust and like him? Don't criticize yourself. Take what is good and make it better. Take what needs improvement and fine-tune it. See yourself as others see you and make yourself into the image of success. *If you look and feel successful, you will be!*

CREATIVE THINKING

1. WHY BE CREATIVE AND HOW IS IT DONE?

It is not possible to solve today's problems with yesterday's solutions if the circumstances are no longer the same. We need a new way to generate ideas and we can do so by thinking creatively. It is great to have knowledge, but it is what we do with the knowledge that counts. Creative thinking is the ability to look at something that everyone else looks at and see it differently. It is the ability to find a different use for the object or change the perspective of how that object or situation is generally utilized. Sometimes it takes an awakening or a shaking up to get us out of our routines. Most of what we do in life is done automatically. By doing something differently, a new perspective is gained.

Try this exercise and see how it feels. Clasp your hands together, interlacing your fingers. Notice which thumb is on the top and which pinky is on the bottom. Now separate your hands and interlace them in the opposite way making sure that the other thumb is on top and the other pinky is on the bottom. It probably took you longer to figure it out the second time and it may have felt unnatural. We get used to doing things a certain way and get into a rut. Try dressing in a different order, sleeping on the other side of the bed, or brushing your teeth with the opposite hand. It's these kinds of things that shake you out of a routine, make you think differently and get a new perspective.

Much of our thinking is geared toward one answer, when in fact, it may be the third or fourth one that is more creative. So instead of thinking of *the* right answer, think in terms of answers. When there is only one idea or one solution, we can't compare it to anything so we won't know its strengths or weaknesses. When we are blocked, we tend to think harder and constrict our thinking even more. Being creative lets many ideas come into play. You never know where these ideas will lead to no matter how silly they seem. Big ideas never just come about. They grow from small ideas that are made bigger and more elaborate, so look at the worth of every small idea and see what can be done with it.

Remember, it is what you do with your knowledge that counts. Think in terms of many correct answers, shake up your routines to gain a new perspective and ask a question in a different way. To say that the day is partly cloudy gives a different connotation than saying that the day is partly sunny. Try changing your perspectives in as many ways as possible and see how many various viewpoints you can come up with in the course of a day. You will start being more creative in every aspect and have fun while doing it.

YOUR TRUE CHARACTER

If you devote all your strength to those things which you are suited for, something will tell you that you are in keeping with your real character. When you feel that you must accomplish something in a given field, you have then found your calling for the present time. Apply all of your concentration to those goals and you will sense the value of your work and the value of your own life. There is no calling when you make no effort, but your creativity increases when you flow with the tide instead of against it.

When you are good at the things you like, you are able to make progress in what you are doing. If you don't like what you are doing, it is difficult to concentrate your mind on it. Progress in things you do not like is slow because you cannot achieve a state of mind and body connectedness. You must achieve this type of unification and then utilize the highest of your abilities *to make it happen*.

DEVELOPING NEW IDEAS

2. HOW TO DEVELOP NEW IDEAS AND GAIN DIFFERENT PERSPECTIVES.

There are two different methods of thinking. One is called brain-storming. This type of thinking is designed to create a maximum number of possibilities and covers a wide area of ideas. It is the kind of thinking that you want to do in the development of ideas. The other kind of thinking is called focused thinking. This method has definite right and wrong answers, it is precise and the focus is narrow. Once you have generated all the ideas you want in the brain-storming stage, you now would use focused thinking to access and execute the idea. Too often focused thinking is used instead of brain-storming in the development of ideas and, therefore, many ideas are never thought of. If diffused thinking is done in the application stage, the ideas will not be carried out. Be aware of when to use each kind of thinking to facilitate your creativeness.

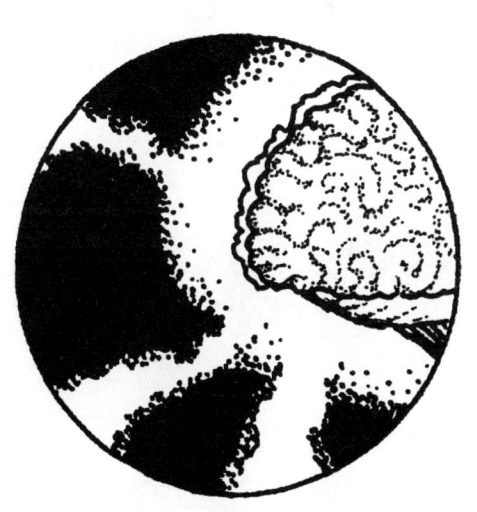

METAPHORS

Metaphors make ideas easier to understand. For instance, finish these sentences with one word:

My life is like a _____.
My job is like a _____.
My boss is like a _____.
My relationship is like a _____.
My health is like a _____.

Add any other topic you want. At a glance you will immediately get feedback as to how you feel about each area and what needs more attention or change.

Another way to gain different perspectives is to ask "just suppose" questions. Just suppose we lived to be 100? Just suppose we had three million dollars? Just suppose money grew on trees? Just suppose you could live on the moon? How would you answer these questions? How would it affect your thinking, and your life if it were so? These types of questions seem absurd, but they do generate a different point of view causing us to access differently. See how many of these questions you could come up with and what kinds of answers they generate.

❈ ❈ ❈

TAKING RISKS

To generate new ideas we must take risks. Most of us don't like to do this, because we can fail, and it does not feel safe. We feel at our best when we succeed and that occurs when we are already familiar with the activity; yet we only learn when we risk and stretch beyond our comfort zone. If you don't succeed, use it as a learning experience and try it another way. Be creative and gain various points of view. Try risking at least once a day. One advertising agency doesn't like more than a 15% success rate of new ideas at any given time or they feel that they are just doing a variation of what already exists and that they are not being creative. The rearrangement of existing substances cannot be called true creativity. No outflow of energy can take place without an inflow. We take the inflow of energy and use that to create what does not yet exist.

Be creative and gain various points of view. Try risking at least once a day, use your "just suppose" questions, metaphors, brain-storm and focused methods of thinking. Creativity is the result of new ideas and different perspectives. You have it all. Just start doing it and notice what happens in your life.

3. YOU MUST GO BEYOND INTELLIGENCE TO BECOME MORE CREATIVE.

To go beyond intelligence takes creative thinking. We must think differently or the result will just be a variation of what already is. See if everything you think is valid. Too often we think in a certain way because it has worked in the past. Validate the fact that the idea or concept is still useful to you or you will be utilizing ideas that are now obsolete if the original purpose is gone.

Sometimes a point of view is cast in cement because our ego is attached to it. Visualize the whole picture to get a different perspective and to see if your point of view holds up. By getting other views, you can tell the strengths and weakness of yours. If it does not hold up, be flexible, let go, and create another idea that will suit your present needs.

Success and failure stem from the same root. What can produce success at one time can produce failure at another. Creative people take chances and learn from their mistakes. So take the risks, become more creative, and know that *success is in the making.*

SELF-ESTEEM

It is usually not beneficial to criticize or praise another person; rather, it is in the person's best interest to criticize or praise what he has *done*. For example, when a secretary misspells the same word for the fourth time, don't say, "I can't believe you are so forgetful." Rather, think of a way to help her associate the word so that it doesn't happen again. Conversely, if she does something well, don't say how proud you are of her, but how proud she must be of herself. Always reinforce the positives and strengthen the weaknesses.

The idea in the first case is to disapprove of the person's behavior without disapproving of the person, and in the second case, to allow the person to conclude that she must be competent for having done something worthwhile.

Lack of self-esteem is commonly associated with depression, anxiety, hostility, difficulty in adapting to new circumstances and reluctance to make an effort. Psychologists have linked low self-esteem to disruptive and antisocial behavior, difficulty in making friends, abuse of drugs, alcohol, and negative reactions from other people. A person who lacks self-esteem can be caught in a vicious cycle: "I am no good. I am going to fail. Therefore, I won't try. Then I'll have an excuse for failing."

When self-esteem is high, a person is unlikely to blame himself for failure or rejection and he is able to put the situation into proper perspective, instead.

PROCESS TO BOLSTER SELF-ESTEEM

Experts say there are a number of things people could do to bolster their self-esteem:

1. FOCUS ON YOUR POTENTIAL, NOT YOUR LIMITATIONS.

2. DEVOTE YOURSELF TO SOMETHING YOU DO WELL.

Many people with talent never realize their potential because they don't make the effort to develop their skill. Don't compare yourself to others who are already successful and then give up in frustration.

3. SEE YOURSELF AS SUCCESSFUL.

Rid yourself of the negative messages. Use visualization and picture yourself succeeding. Do this imaging over and over again until the feeling becomes ingrained within you.

4. BREAK AWAY FROM OTHER PEOPLE'S EXPECTATIONS.

Don't try to be someone you are not. Attempts to impress others nearly always fail.

★ ★ ★

PATHWAYS FOR SUCCESS
SEVEN WINNING BEHAVIORS YOU NEED FOR SUCCESS

1. In order to reach your true potential, you must have an all consuming passion. If the passion is not there, it is easy to give up when the project becomes difficult. It is only that passion that keeps you going even when the going gets tough.

2. You must have the belief of who you are, what you can become and realize that whatever your mind can conceive, your mind can achieve. Know that your mind is the most complex computer and you have no limitations.

3. Incorporate a strategy of organizing resources to work to your potential. Seek out other people who have accomplished similar goals. It may be in totally different areas, but their strategy may be adaptable and can be utilized to suit your needs.

4. Having clear values and knowing what really matters in your life will make it easier to manifest what you want. If your goals are not clear, sift out what you don't want and see what is left. The more specific you are about what you do want, makes it easier for you to accomplish it.

5. You must have the energy and vibrancy for success. Make sure you are not just achieving an isolated incident to be accomplished, but that you are designing a life.

6. You must have the ability to develop a deep rapport with others. This is not only great to use for networking, but to have as a resource and support group as well.

7. In order to produce new results you must have mastery of communication both from within and without. Goals are only signposts pointing you in a certain direction. Thoughts have no power over us unless we give in to them. They are only words strung together. The sort of meaning

they have to us is what we choose to give them. Only choose to think thoughts that nourish and support you and you will feel strong.

Try this exercise: Monitor your thoughts for one hour and notice the words you think about yourself. It is said that we think one negative or hurtful remark about ourselves every 60 seconds. Like: "Am I dumb!" "How could I have done that?" "How stupid of me." Multiply these negative thoughts times the hours in a day, the days in a year and times your age, to see how many times you have reinforced negatives in your life. Starting now—become aware of those thoughts and start reinforcing the positive.

SIX KEY BELIEFS FOR SUCCESS THAT ALL SUCCESSFUL PEOPLE KNOW

1. There are no coincidences. Everything happens for a reason. Take the results and find out what you can learn from them. There are no such things as failures—only results. Wrong-doing is only the result of wrong-thinking. By changing your thinking, the results will change; therefore, proper thinking will produce the results you want.

2. People who fear failure develop a fear of what might not work in advance. Therefore, they feel it is pointless to take action as they are not going to succeed anyway. They sabotage their own success and never develop a success mentality. The *purpose* that you have is much more important than the *object* that is being pursued. So if you understand why you want to be rich rather than how to do it, you will have enough reasons to accomplish it.

3. Take responsibility for whatever happens. We usually take credit for our successes and blame others for our failures. Whatever happens—own up to it.

4. People are your greatest resource so form a successful support team and network.

5. Regard your work as play. We relax, let our guard down and become much more creative during play. These

are the aspects that should be included into work. The process must be fun to make the results worthwhile.

6. Success in anything can only be accomplished by commitment. Just being interested wanes after a period of time. The mind and body must be in conjunction with one another to pursue success. A person who is more committed will surpass a person who has more talent but is not as committed.

To summarize, be committed, convert work into play, form your support team, take responsibility, understand your purpose, and change your thinking to get the success you deserve.

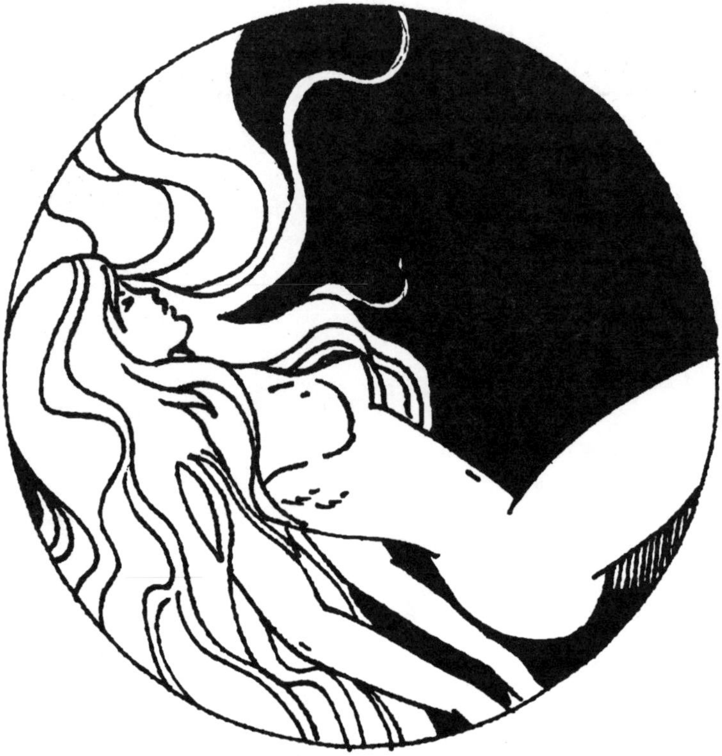

-RELATIONSHIPS-
THE MATING GAME

FOUR MISCONCEPTIONS OF LOVE

Love is the ability to do very well on your own, but enjoying it more with this special other person. One misconception is that falling in love makes you happy and whole. It is foolish to think that falling in love joins both people as one and that loneliness disappears. When each person has different needs and wants, they will find conflict or initiate the work of real loving. This real love occurs when we act lovingly despite the fact that we don't feel like it.

Try this exercise: Draw a line vertically down the middle of a page and write down your priorities on one side of the line and your partner's priorities on the other. See where they match and where there are differences. Then take another piece of paper and make three columns. In column #1 write the aspects you must have in a relationship; in column #2 write what you would like to have, but you could live without; in column #3 write down what you absolutely can't tolerate. Have your partner do this on another piece of paper. Now take all of these lists and compare what you have in common with your partner, what can be changed and compromised with, and where both of your priorities are. If you love going out and your partner does not, you have a major compromise to make. Love is not the joining of two individuals into one, but a separateness encouraging growth in each other.

Another misconception is that there is only one perfect mate and that they will satisfy each other's needs forever. Each person grows at a different rate and sometimes the growth pattern encompasses various interests and hobbies. If you find yourself committed to a relationship that is no longer romantic or fulfilling, try to see what is bonding you two together. Encourage the "winged life" in yourself and in your partner, but there must be respect and love to nourish or you are holding on to something that no longer exists.

Another misconception is that dependency is love. Love is free choice. Two people love each other when they are capable of living without each other, but choose to live with each other. When one says that "I can't live without him," that is being a parasite—not a lover. The only true closeness in the relationship is for individual growth and growth as a couple.

The fourth fallacy is that love is a feeling. Love is an action. It is volitional rather than emotional. The person who truly loves does so because of a decision to love. It is actually a commitment to be loving whether or not the loving feeling is present. The common tendency to confuse love with the feeling of love allows people to be open to self-deception. Know the difference between lust and love. In love, we extend ourselves to the nurturing of ourselves and another so it is commitment. By being aware that both of you are committed, you could then have a lusting and loving relationship that grows.

STRENGTHENING YOUR INTIMATE RELATIONSHIP

Love takes plenty of attention. One way to pay attention is to listen. Listening well is hard because our attention span is generally very short. Many times we come away with little of what the speaker said because we didn't concentrate or we have our own ideas about the subject and tune out. True listening is a skill and we must set aside our own prejudices and desires to experience the speaker's point of view. It temporarily involves the total acceptance of the other person. When this happens, the speaker and listener appreciate each other more. True listening is love in action.

Love also encompasses courage. Courage is not the absence of fear. It is taking action in spite of fear, and in many cases, involves risk. The risk is that the person may move away from you and leave you more lonely than you were before, that you may get hurt, or that the person may let you down. Risking allows you to live life fully and not just exist. By risking, you choose options to grow and the relationship will grow. Do things and act in ways that satisfy you. If you do them to satisfy someone else, the commitment is superficial. Commitment is the foundation of a loving relationship. One can foster growth only through a relationship of consistency. Couples cannot talk or resolve issues of dependency and independence, freedom and fidelity without the security of knowing that the discussion of these topics will not in itself destroy the relationship.

The greatest risk of love is the act of confrontation which is saying, "I am right and you are wrong." The act of shooting from the hip comes quite easily and hurts. Constructive criticism doesn't come easily as issues and motives must be examined or the criticism produces more resentment than growth. In any good relationship you are each others' best critics, but to confront someone with something that he can't handle is a waste of time. You must be able to relate on your partner's level. Exercising power with love is a fragile task.

Love is spontaneous; yet it is disciplined. Loving behavior is expected in such a way to contribute to each other's growth. One must constantly adjust feelings to meet the situation. Love is separateness and the distinction between oneself and the other is always maintained. So remember—love takes plenty of attention, encompasses courage and risk, needs commitment, constructive criticism, and the flexibility to grow. Take the freedom to explore, to grow and to change with life. You are responsible for your own happiness. Take charge and do it!

THREE TECHNIQUES FOR MAKING YOUR RELATIONSHIP GREAT

Repressing anger only causes anxiety and can create illness and disease. The best way to alleviate this is to communicate to your partner what is bothering you.

Technique #1. Have a particular place and time everyday or evening set aside for just the two of you. Don't just talk about what you did that day, but discuss all the feelings that went along with it as well. You might tell him how much you loved him when he did or said thus and such, and how great it made you feel, but how much you disliked what he did in the afternoon and how much it hurt you. Go into all specifics and talk it out thoroughly. Talking is a form of release. Getting out all these feelings will allow a neutralization of these past events. This way nothing gets built up or blown out of proportion and a clean slate is established to start anew. It is much harder to erase a slate when days of building anger upon anger is allowed. Remember to always criticize with love and that only comes when you self-examine the issues and try to be objective rather than emotional while discussing them.

Technique #2. When something is bothering your partner, just allow him to talk and when he is through, repeat what he said. Sometimes we think we hear one thing, when in actuality, something else was inferred. By being on the listening end, a different perspective of the problem can be brought out. When he is totally finished, then it is your turn to talk and let him repeat what you said. In many cases this allows both individuals to experience what the other person felt and resolves the conflict much quicker.

Technique #3. This method allows you to become your own sounding board. It enables you to detach from an emotional situation, and as a result, you view situations more objectively rather than emotionally. Choose an incident or event that really bothered you. Now close your eyes if you are in a situation that allows you to do so, get in a comfortable position, take a couple of deep breaths and imagine the incident from beginning to end. Don't judge or say, "I should have said that or could have done this," but go through the entire scenario as if it were a character on this screen that resembled you, but was not you. When the entire picture show is over, open your eyes. Notice how you feel. Viewing it this way allows you to be objective. When you are detached emotionally, you are able to see whether you have been upset over someone else's problem. It is a great tool for becoming your own sounding board. If the incident is deeply ingrained within you, do this viewing a few more times until you get tired of the picture. At this point you have become the master and it no longer has the same, if any, power over you. The result is that you can now act from strength rather than react from emotions.

CREATING THE RELATIONSHIP YOU DESERVE

The easiest way to leave a relationship is to shut down emotionally, "emotional anesthesia." Most people really don't listen to what the other person is saying. We stay with our own opinions and automatically shut down to other ideas. Love supposedly joins both people together and loneliness disappears. This is a fallacy as you must have your own self-esteem and the other person is beneficial when he complements your actions, feelings and attitudes. It is important to search for what is missing in yourself before looking on the outside for another relationship. Why should someone else love you if you don't have that same feeling or regard for yourself? Opposites attract because we look for the qualities in the other person that we wish we had. We think that we will then feel completed by being in a relationship with that person. Non-fulfillment occurs with the realization that those qualities are still not ours unless we change and make them ours.

A relationship is not a promise of what can never be, but taking it where it is now and growing with that as a base. If you change the behaviors of your partner into what you want him to be, he is no longer the same person that you were attracted to in the first place. Be involved because you want to be, not because you have to be. You are responsible for your own pleasure. A good relationship supports change and doesn't let fear of the unknown stop one's own growth. In fact, fear can be used as a motivator for change and growth, rather than as an inhibiting factor. A relationship is not something you own or possess—you are in it.

Resentment breaks down positive beliefs and creates a variety of fears. Resentment can be defined as a feeling of indignant displeasure at some person, act, or remark regarded as causing injury or insult. When you forgive, you give up resentment. You may not like the behavior of the person, but you can release the anger toward the individual.

Think of the experiences, situations, or people that have caused you to feel resentment and visualize a way that you can forgive their actions. This creates an inner peace within you and allows contentment without this nagging hostility that one just carries as excess baggage. The feeling is heavy, burdensome and unnecessary. If the solution is not to be involved with the person again, then it is a conscious decision and you are acting instead of reacting. The choice to forgive and not to retaliate is the start of transformation.

Get clear with what you do want or you will be looking for old attractions. Many times a new relationship will create the same problems as the old one because the patterns of attractions which didn't work before are still unresolved within you. This results in attracting the same energy that you have been trying to avoid. You then get upset with yourself for doing the same things again. What is most important is to remember that you deserve your own love and respect. You can learn your lessons in life without hating yourself for your problems. No one can love you more than you love yourself or you will push him away. If you love someone more than they love themselves, you will be rejected.

Create a self-esteem profile. List all of the qualities both negative and positive associated with yourself. Then create one for your significant other. See where they match up and what aspects need strengthening. Self-acceptance is the first step to self-esteem. Self-respect is the second step. You will never lose anything that is for your highest good.

You can only *experience* your true essence as your mind cannot measure the fullness of who you are. Sometimes you have to fall apart to find out how together you really are. Use all of these experiences as learning tools and don't get discouraged. Confusion is good as it is a loosening up of an old pattern and allows a new perspective to take hold.

Energy follows thought. As you ponder words with great feeling, know that the energy of this desire is penetrating your consciousness to do the creative work necessary to make your thought a reality. For the next two weeks state what you want every hour. Remember, what you ask will happen, so be positive that it is what you want in your life as you are likely to receive it. Ask yourself some of these types of questions to find out what you really do want.

1. What are your values?
2. What are some of the things that you believe in?
3. In detail describe the important relationships in your life.
4. What is their relationship to you?
5. What do you want in a relationship?

By probing into specific areas, you can see where the strengths lie and what parts need more attention. By affirming that you choose to realize a dynamic, vibrant and loving relationship, your attention is focused to this type and any other sort will not feel right. Your unconscious will attract what is best for you at this present time—so be specific. Tell yourself that you accept the fulfillment of this desire mentally, physically and emotionally and that you feel the energy of this idea entering into your consciousness. You now have conceived of the perfect idea of a perfect relationship. Because you have accepted all the aspects of what this relationship means, you now have a conscious link as well. See yourself enjoying this relationship and awakening to this energy. Feel, see, and smell the presence of this individual. See the oneness of this partnership; yet the individuality for growth. Enjoy it for what it is, not for what it could be. You will then feel a bond of love that is complete and the sensation of separateness will disappear as you join another energy frequency that can expand and boost your own. Just be cognizant that you can be fine without this person, but that it is your choice to be there because it is enhancing your life at this time. Just don't ever give up your freedom as you are still the most important person for you.

Memories and past beliefs of what "was" is exactly that—in the past. These concepts are not viable unless you can utilize them in the present.

Flexibility is growth and stiffness is death. A baby comes into the world totally flexible and is vibrantly alive.

As we grow older, many of our joints and muscles, as well as our ideas, tend to be less flexible and they are actually in the process of dying. Remain fluid in all aspects of life and continue to mature with experience and change.

It is through these experiences that we achieve mastery over the world of illusion. Our perceptions are the reality upon which we base our belief system. Too many times we recharge our battery of consciousness with fear, depression and conflict, rather than with faith, happiness and unconditional love. It is with this positive recharging that relationships bond and strengthen. We are more comfortable worrying about the future of this relationship than in experiencing a joyful life now. Too often we are constricted in this polluted comfort zone until we find something more interesting and more important than our fears, depressions, conflicts, and concerns about what may go wrong in the future. If we are ready to experience freedom, then our belief systems must reflect our power as this power is in direct proportion to the strength of our beliefs.

ELIMINATING FEAR

Fear is the root cause of many of our problems. Monitor your thoughts, words, and actions to realize how often fear is self-affirmed. We are afraid of lacking—afraid of abundance—afraid of success—afraid of failure—afraid of sickness—and it continues. Recognize that there is nothing to fear. It is merely being afraid of illusions, and illusions are not facts. When you have no fear, then somewhere in your mind you know you are connected to a higher macrocosm from which you can draw in more energy and intelligence. When you do fear, you are just drawing in from your own strength. When that is not enough, there is no where else to reach. When we fear anything, we are projecting a consciousness operating out of a faulty belief system. Out of fear we create images that crystallize into forms and experiences which we judge to be bad. This escalates the vibration of fear to a higher level.

Fear is an energy block. This negative energy called "fear" is the result of errant thoughts which we have developed into belief systems. These beliefs are externalized and mirror your convictions. Change a partial belief to an absolute conviction to alter your outside reality. Belief is a point of conscious energy pulsating to a certain vibration within a sphere of its own realm of possibility and probability. There are varying degrees of beliefs with the externalization reflecting the exact degree of the belief you hold. When a belief is total and complete, it would rate a score of ten on a scale of 0-10, and total disbelief would score zero. Apply this scale to specific aspects of your relationships and upscale the areas that need it.

The act of thinking is different from actually believing. Thoughts and ideas can become beliefs and positioned in our consciousness as an absolute reality only if it remains uncontradicted. How many times during a day do we contradict what we really want? To manifest an idea or concept, it must first appear both interesting and important, and it must excite and stimulate our interest. When something appeals to us so vividly that we accept it, we must fill our minds with it. Only then does it become real for us and we believe it. The interest must stimulate the emotion and when the feeling reaches the degree of passion, it is regarded as a belief in the mind. We then must act as if it were real, and keep acting as though it were real, until it grows into such a connection with our life that our direction will make it real. If it is that perfect mate that you want, go through this process with as much detail as possible and have that person come into your life.

CHARACTERISTICS FOR HAPPINESS

There are characteristics of ourselves and our loved ones that should be recognized in order to curtail inevitable problems. One such aspect is that of poor problem solving. These are the people that wait for the problem to go away instead of handling it. The difficulty can only be resolved when you take responsibility for it. Too many times we play the victim and expect others to solve the problem since they created it in the first place. The objection we have in accepting responsibility for our behavior is due to avoiding the pain of the consequences of that behavior. It is important to note that if a person is unwilling to change or to accept responsibility, the individual will feel impotent.

Another characteristic is rigidity and inflexibility in thinking and behavior. The more clearly we see the reality of the world, the better we can deal with it. Many people stop filtering any information unless it conforms to their map of reality so their views of reality are sketchy, narrow, and misleading. Views should always have the capacity to change when new information is introduced or the person will be defending an outmoded opinion. Truth can only be known when we risk and constantly expose our reality to the criticism and challenge of others. If your partner's opinions are cast in cement, you will have a hard time expressing anything to the contrary.

Also be aware of a person who processes by deletion. This is an individual that selectively pays attention to certain aspects of an experience and overlooks or omits all other information. Another process is that of distortion. This occurs when we make misrepresentations of reality. We can over generalize or be too specific for the generalization we have concluded. When given the same stimulus, people will have various responses as to the way they process the information. This is individualized. Knowing how you and your partner process information will enable you both to have a smoother path. JUST REALIZE THAT EACH PROBLEM WAS ONCE A SOLUTION TO A PREVIOUS PROBLEM. Life goes on with more problems and creative solutions.

Are you or your partner hesitant about losing your freedom due to commitment? The two terms are actually synonymous as the more freely you choose, the more appropriate your choices. Then your commitment is out of choice, not obligation. Until you are committed to your own well-being, the possibility of commitment to a relationship is premature. Since commitment is based on desire, not on a sense of duty, what some people call freedom is really only escapism. Sometimes the label "free spirit" only paralyzes the person in not choosing and promotes him to just drift through life in the same recurrent patterns as before. It is easier to commit whole-heartedly to a partnership when each can maintain individual freedom and not be afraid of being swallowed up or smothered by the other person. An ideal partner is a friend whose passion for you increases the more he experiences your diversity.

EVALUATING YOUR RELATIONSHIP

Make sure that you celebrate and acknowledge the successes of your relationship. Too often the negative aspects are harped on and the positive points are not even mentioned. Focus on what you love about each other and do less criticism. If you do criticize, make sure it is done with love and to be helpful, not hurtful. By recognizing all the good, a success mentality is created and the relationship has a strong foundation because of this mentality. Then the foundation is thought to be solid with a few flaws that need strengthening, rather than weak with a few good parts.

Communication is a necessary tool for maintaining a good relationship. Ninety percent of all communication is non-verbal and only ten percent is verbal. We learn through body language, facial expressions, actions and intuition. Listen to each other every way you can. When you only want to make him happy, and he wants the same for you, then it is easy to give because you know you will be receiving at least as much as you are putting forth.

Evaluate both of your self-esteem levels. When one person needs help in this area, he may sabotage success and look for problems even when there is none. This is done unconsciously as he may be trying to destroy what he fears he doesn't deserve. Meanwhile, you may become his scapegoat. What is resisted, persists.

Self-love, self-respect, and self-esteem are all necessary for a successful relationship. Be cognizant of where you both are in this area. The more you know about each other, the better everything will be. There is no reason for boredom or stagnation in a growing relationship unless you have stopped growing. Using past experiences and taking them to new heights are exciting and keep the partnership interesting. The more you trust each other, the more vulnerable you become. True loving comes with trust as your defenses are not necessary and you can truly experience this person without the fear of being hurt.

Don't worry about loss. Some people will do anything to hang on to a relationship that is no longer viable or healthy for them. If someone leaves you, it will only make room for someone better. No one leaves if he is happy and complete. Be with someone because you both want to be with each other, not because you feel you *need* each other. Love only heals and rejuvenates you if the elements are right for the both of you.

Make a check list of what makes you happy and be specific in what you want, whom you want, and where you want it. Ask and you shall receive! You always manifest what you want so you might as well do it consciously and get precisely what you do want. You create what you believe to be true at that moment. Be able to change and manifest whatever you need as you grow, evolve, and mature. Having a vision allows you to take the necessary steps to achieve it. What you focus in your mind, expands in your experience.

List any other characteristics or qualities that you have, want to have, or want to change. Then think of ways to strengthen or gain what you wish to ingrain in your behavior.

Take responsibility and take action! The first step is always the hardest, but it all becomes easier when you have a direction to follow. When you know who you are and like it, then what you want becomes clearer.

Conflict shows up in many various ways. It is neither positive or negative. *It just is*. Like stress, it is what you do with the conflict that counts. Learning and growing from it are goals for resolution. Resolving conflict is rarely about who is right. It is about the acknowledgment and appreciation of differences. Conflict is not a contest although some couples make it seem so. Too many times we just try to prove rightness and the more "right" each is, the more separate you become and more limited in the ability to attain peace.

Discovery is wonderful. Open yourself up to all that your partner and the world have to offer. Become vulnerable with the trust that you will not be hurt. Let new information come into your belief systems so that you can extend your boundaries into new fields of endeavor. When you have created a set of beliefs, you have excluded everything else. Limitations come from inflexibility and limited knowledge and experience. The key to achieving excellence and reaching our full potential as an individual and as a couple, is the willingness to take the risks to explore our limits.

Whenever you deal with another person, be aware of when you become judgmental. It is vital to communicate feelings and opinions, not just positions on the issue. To avoid conflict, concentrate on asking questions and listening, rather than giving your own answers and solutions. Listening increases rapport as you are acknowledging that the other person is worth listening to. It may also create new options to get to solutions in ways that you may not have conceived before. Being willing to listen and to change also allow you to recognize different perspectives, and create greater possibilities to see the entire picture or vision. You then have a comparison as to how your issues or solutions hold up in the context of others. It is only through comparison with many ideas that you will know the strengths and weaknesses of your own. Polls have been taken with the result that there is an average of ten criticisms to one compliment in any given time frame with another person—even self-criticism.

CO-CREATING

Co-creating with your partner takes listening, understanding and a commitment to discover solutions together. Once a common goal is identified, your concentration can be placed on solutions rather than differences. If your goal is clear, taking action happens naturally. When it is a vision that you both want, then the work to make it happen seems more like play.

Co-creating is an exciting experience, as it is a compounding of ideas to form new experiences for the two of you. Think of a tomato plant. In order to get hundreds of tomatoes, you need to start with a small seed. That seed doesn't look like a tomato plant, but you plant it in fertile soil, water it and let the sun shine on it. You then watch it grow from a tiny shoot to a plant. You pull away the weeds and see all those tomatoes that came from that one seed.

It is the same for you. The soil you plant in is your unconscious mind. The seed is the new thought, and the whole new experience is in this tiny seed. You keep watering it with positive thoughts. You weed the garden by pulling out the negative thoughts and then watch it manifest itself because of all the care and nurturing it has been receiving.

We switch attitudes, go through mood swings, and can exude various personalities in the course of a day. We can go through various mind-sets according to the circumstances that are filtering into our lives. Some of these mental sets are destructive and others are extremely beneficial. Therefore, it is important to recognize what you and your partner are thinking, and how you are reacting, so that you can switch into modes that are more positive. Many times we don't even recognize what we are thinking until we are deeply entrenched into depression and need help.

FIVE COMMON MIND-SETS

The first three mind-sets are uncomfortable and damaging to self-esteem and well-being. They create a continual loss of energy, an increase in fear and separation, and a feeling of struggle.

1. Just getting by—This mentality believes that you better get all that you can because there is a great lack of resources. If you don't get it first, someone else will. This is a drain on your energy as all your output is used up in maintaining this idea of scarcity.

2. Entropy—This mind-set believes that everything is on a downhill trend. The world is in a terrible state, we are getting old, things aren't what they used to be, and everything only gets worse. In this state of mind, action appears pointless and we just let things happen to us—the victim role.

3. Destruction—When we are in the "entropy" mode for a length of time, we can perceive our path and energy as being stuck. This is when we consider ourselves a failure. We pull others down into this scenario.

These next two mind-sets are positive and what you want to switch into.

1. Success—When we are feeling better, we experience life as being full of choices and opportunities. We can utilize stress as a motivator. There is an abundance of energy in this mode.

2. Beyond Success—This is the most balanced state as you cooperate with others, see the world as supportive, and realize that there is abundance for everyone.

Recognizing what mental state you or your partner are in, allows you both to help each other. The main key here is awareness. Whenever someone is aware of how he is thinking, feeling and acting, the process of changing into another state becomes easier.

THERAPEUTIC TOUCH

WHY THERAPEUTIC TOUCH WORKS

One of the most significant breakthroughs in nursing education has been the introduction and acceptance of healing through touch. Used today in both traditional and alternative medicine, Therapeutic Touch is a highly effective technique for healing yourself and others. The process of Therapeutic Touch is accomplished through energy transference.

This field of healing is an outgrowth of the laying on of hands. Energy as a life force has been an accepted fact in Eastern countries for many decades. Western philosophy is just becoming aware of such phenomena and realizing it's merits. Eastern literature states that people have "prana" which is a Sanskrit word for energy or the life force. Normally, healthy people have an excess of prana; yet in the East, people believe that those who are ill have a deficit of this energy. It is also said that this prana can be transferred from one person to another. This is the same energy that is called "chi" energy which is used in t'ai chi. This energy is synonymous with the "ki" force which is used in aikido and karate.

The reason that energy can be transferred is due to the fact that you can be likened to a free flowing battery. A radio antenna picks up a certain frequency and is able to produce sounds. A television antenna tunes into a frequency to produce pictures. Since everything is energy, energy is omnipresent. In the same mode the healer becomes a human antenna and can channel this universal energy to another who is deficient and needs it. The person receiving the energy being transferred from the healer is called the receiver. When deficit of energy, the receiver accepts this energy boost which is then sent to the areas that need to be healed. *The patient always heals himself!* The healer merely provides the energy for the receiver. To tune energy to yourself converts all the energy in your body to your own vibration. Tuning energy to another person allows you to give him energy which does not have to be converted to his own vibration and it can be used immediately. Resonance occurs when there is an energy transfer between two oscillating fields. Since energy flows from a high to a low potential, subtle energy of the proper frequency will be accepted to shift the body into a new equilibrium point of health.

The general vitality of an individual is an indirect reflection of the level of functioning of the immune system. When the human body is weakened, it oscillates at a less harmonious frequency than when it is healthy. This abnormal frequency reflects a general state of cellular energetic imbalance within the physical body. When a weakened individual is unable to shift his energetic mode to the needed frequency which allows his immune system to properly defend the body, energy transference may help. This energy allows the cellular systems to resonate in the proper vibrational modes resulting in the elimination of toxicities of the illness and returns the bio-energy systems to a new level of homeostasis.

KIRLIAN PHOTOGRAPHY

Kirlian, a Russian botanist, was the first person to use infrared photography to actually prove that energy fields exist. He took infrared pictures of a leaf and noticed that in the photo a glow was produced around the contour of the leaf. He had no idea what this glow meant. He then cut off a portion of the leaf and took the picture. The same glow appeared in the photo; but the glow's contour was as if the leaf was whole and not cut. For the next few months he continued taking pictures of the same cut leaves. He noticed that the glow started to fade and conform to the cut leaf's outline. Kirlian realized that this was an energy configuration, and that the energy patterns reacted as if the leaf was in its entirety. This was a very important breakthrough because it explained "phantom limb pain." When a person lost an arm, a finger, or a leg etc. in an accident, he might claim that he still felt the actual pain of that missing limb. The person was often sent to a therapist, was told that it was all in his mind, and would then be treated for a mental aberration which was termed phantom limb pain. Kirlian photography was proof that energy remains in the same energy pattern that had existed when the physical appendage was a reality. With this new evidence, the doctors started to treat the patient differently. The patient's pain was now treated as being real. Mental health comes with knowing that there is a reason for pain and that it is not just psychosomatic.

As I was explaining this in a radio interview, a man called in to profusely thank me for making him feel normal. He had been complaining of pain due to a finger that he lost on a job site three months previously. The doctor was prescribing Valium and said the pain was all due to nerves. Just having a decent explanation created the way for this man to feel sane.

HISTORY OF TOUCH

During the 1960's Colonel Oskar Estebany of the Hungarian cavalry was healing animals, especially horses. He became so well renowned for his work that many of the cavalrymen would bring their horses to him for healing. Estebany magnetized bandages and put it on the affected surfaces of the horse. He recognized that if the hurt area was put into an electrical field, the area would heal itself faster. One day a neighbor's child became extremely ill and the family could not reach a doctor. Estebany was asked to help, and although he had never treated humans before, he did, and the child got better. Then Estebany continued to work with both people and animals until he retired from the cavalry. He then decided to continue his work for research purposes, and after a series of events, he found himself in Canada where he joined a group with Dora Kunz in researching the act of healing.

Dora was working in Canada at the same time that Estebany was working in Hungary. She was healing people with energy transfers. Her unique abilities to perceive subtle energies around living beings enabled her to work with medical doctors and scientists in research.

Delores Krieger was a student of Dora's and she became part of that same study group in Canada with Dora and Estebany. Delores eventually designed a course of study for New York University called Frontiers in Nursing: The Actualization of Potential for Therapeutic Human Field Interaction. It was the first class of its kind in the United States with a fully accredited curriculum for the master's degree. Over 7,000 professionals and nurses have since taken this course. The students who have taken this have been affectionately known as "Krieger's Krazies." Many doctors are aware that the method works; people are getting healthier in a much shorter period of time. More importantly, patients are leaving the hospitals quicker. So even if the medical field is not sure as to why it works, the results with the patients that receive Therapeutic Touch have been impressive.

During healing sessions in Canada, Estebany had amazing results with patients. When he put his hands on them, people were getting better, quicker. He was able to change the ionization of water under laboratory conditions. In conjunction with his healing, Dora described the healee's pathology and it was as if she were perceiving the patient's inner functions and dysfunctions. Their work was so impressive that the Menninger Foundation gave them a grant to continue their work. They went to New York to further their research.

CASE STUDIES

Therapeutic Touch does not depend upon belief. It works whether you have faith in it or not. I have treated patients in critical care units who are comatose and have no conscious idea that I am treating them; yet the needles on the machines change. One of my clients was hooked up to a respirator and her heart beat was 48 beats per minute. The doctor did not give her long to live. Within 10 minutes of treatment the heart rate was up to 68 beats per minute and whistles started coming out of the respirator. The nurses came running in and deemed it a miracle because those sounds meant that she was breathing well on her own and no longer needed mechanical aid. I came back later that day and gave her another energy transfer. After doing this daily, she was moved into a regular room in the hospital.

Therapeutic Touch treatments may not work if the person needs the illness. It can be his calling card and attention-getter. I had a client whose son brought her to me with chest pains. The doctors had not been able to find out the cause. These symptoms have gone on for years, which coincidentally, was within the same time period that the son got married. All of her hospital and laboratory tests were not showing anything. I scanned her energy field and found no apparent blockages. This woman literally manifested these tremendous pains to keep her son running back to her. It is only in therapy that the causes can be brought out for her to realize what she is doing and why. Sometimes the client will never admit to it and will continue manifesting illness for attention.

Mononucleosis is an illness that manifests within many students during the freshman year at college. One reason for its appearance is that it is basically the first year that he is on his own and must function by himself. On an unconscious level the person is asking for help and wants the security of home. Boom—"mono" comes to the rescue and the child goes home for some tender loving care. Other times that mono is prevalent is during the law boards or the doctoral finals. The student then subconsciously wonders if he can make it, will he pass, and thinks about all the time, money and effort that has been spent. This illness gives just the respite needed until he can mentally get himself back together again.

Another such case involved Tom, a self made man who worked his way up to vice-president of a major corporation. Tom's work record was impeccable. He was bright, creative, productive, always on time and never sick or absent. One month after he was promoted to V.P., he developed a low grade virus. He took a week off to stay in bed and do all the things one needs to do in order to get well. He went back to work and a couple of days later, he had to go back in bed because he was feeling so terrible. The diagnosis was that he had not gotten over this "bug." When this happened a third time, I was called by his wife (who was a student of mine) to come over and help him. Can you surmise what the problem was? Unconsciously this man was going through all kinds of mental games. For instance, the job would entail travel so he would be away from home and family for periods of time. If he made a mistake, others would be watching and waiting to take the job away from him. What if he really did not have the capabilities and everyone would know that he failed. Result—manifest something that would allow the comfort zone to enfold once again. Presto—a virus comes onto the scene. Although this seems very simplistic, the illness is self-created. It is okay to create these symptoms for the body to rest. The danger comes when the individual radiates these illnesses because of habit as it doesn't know any other way to cope. Even when a practitioner does Therapeutic Touch and strengthens the client's energy, he then needs to figure out what will work in the therapy session to enable the patient to understand why these symptoms are happening. Once Tom recognized why, and that is a tricky task as I couldn't just come out and tell him what he was doing, he went back to work and remained there. He became more self-confident, which was the only positive feedback that he needed to end his fears. Once the fears were understood, they could be neutralized.

Every individual case must be handled differently, even if the symptoms are the same. Nothing just goes away without something else taking its place, as nature never just leaves a void. Intellectually, a person may not want to be lonely, but she would have to do something so that this loneliness disappears. It may be in the form of joining a group, going to meetings, or finding a job. Slowly these other things start filling her life and loneliness becomes a thing of the past. It just doesn't happen because you hope for something else; you must *do* something else.

To illustrate the complexities of a case, this one was quite a challenge. Mary called and said she had read about me, thought that I could help her as she was diagnosed as having cancer, that she lived 1/2 hour away, and that she has not driven a car in two years. We made an appointment. Mary showed up and when I opened the door, she said she realized that she had made a mistake and wanted to return home. I told her that she had choices. She could go home immediately, come in and have a drink, or just sit down and talk, or rest for a while before she leaves. She hesitated, said she would come in, but since there was no way I could really help her, she would have a drink and then leave.

Instead of leaving, Mary started talking about her life. Her alcoholic husband left her with her three children when the oldest child was five. One of her teenagers is in jail for drugs, one is an alcoholic, and the third adolescent was just arrested for theft. She lives with her mother (with whom she has a love/hate relationship) and feels guilty about having those feelings. She was a well known opera singer, but didn't sing anymore because she feels that she doesn't deserve to. She doesn't leave the house, keeps the shades pulled down, and orders in anything that is needed. This woman did not think that she even deserved fresh air. She had become a total shut-in for two years.

I asked her only the pertinent questions to keep her talking as she obviously had not spoken to anyone. Ten days before our meeting she found out that she had cancer, and that was the straw that broke it for her. Her body and mind went into fear and she could not eat or sleep or find a place where she was comfortable. I asked her if she would like an energy treatment just to balance her. She said it would be fine as long as I didn't charge her for it as it would then be a professional visit. She exhibited enthusiasm with the feel of energy going through her and even admitted that she felt better afterward. When she realized that she expressed something other than depression, she said it was time to leave.

I asked her how she received her mail and she replied that the mailman delivered it. I said it would be nice to smile at the man and even take a daily walk. She said that she did not need my advice because she knew I couldn't help her. Mary called me a week later and wanted to come over the next day. As I opened the door for her, she was already telling me how ineffectual the advice was as she only smiled at the mailman three times and only went for a walk twice. She knew she would not do what she was told.

Mary talked more and I found out that she loved gardening, but hadn't done it in ages. Before she left, I told her to just go in the garden, dig holes, not to plant anything, and then fill the holes back up. She also said that there was a choral group in her church that was creating a rendition of some opera that she used to sing. I suggested that she sit in at some of the rehearsals (don't give them any advice) and see what it was like.

This time Mary called back in two weeks and wanted to come that same day. She stomped into the house just about yelling how I didn't know what I was doing and that she had to come and tell me how wrong I was. She did go into the garden, and instead of just digging holes, she planted tomatoes. She did go to the choral group and didn't just sit there as I suggested. They were in such need of help, that she became their consultant. She felt that she had to come back just to tell me that none of my methods were useful. She also went back to the doctor and was doing visualizations for part of her cancer therapy.

I related this case study just to show you how individualized and unique every case is. Since Mary processes by opposites, it was clear how to get her to move out of her self-made rut. She never called again, but I did read an article about her being hired as the new opera consultant at the theater of performing arts in her town.

There are many cases that I can delve into to show you that it is not just a matter of doing energy transferences for healing, but a combination of nutrition, exercise and therapy as well. When a client comes in with a tumor, I concentrate on the strengths of the individual and make them stronger. When a person is balanced and strong mentally, emotionally and physically, the illness (in this case—the tumor) stands a good chance of dissipating, as illness cannot live in an environment of strength.

Think of the times that you were ill. The doctors would say that you had low resistance. In actuality you may have been overworked, fatigued and definitely not balanced. That is when you are susceptible to illness.

When I was taking classes at N.Y.U. to become certified in Touch, there were 35 head nurses from all over the U.S. taking the course. One nurse came into the class all excited, reporting that there was a patient in her care at the hospital who was in pain and dying. "Guess what?" she shouted as we shared our experiences. She gave Touch to the patient, and even though the client died, she didn't die in pain. I didn't think that was such a great report at the time, and none of us would pair up with her when we had exercises to do. Only afterwards did we realize that even if we can't save everyone, it's great to be able to ease suffering.

It is important to shield yourself so that you are a free flowing channel and so that you do not pick up any of the patient's symptoms. Refer to the exercises at the end of the chapter to learn how to shield. One of the first times that I was giving a treatment, I didn't shield and felt my energy change to quick flutters. My heart beat faster, my pulse quickened and I felt jittery and uncomfortable. I was exhausted and depleted of energy. All of this resulted because I didn't shield. I had picked up the patient's energy and felt lethargic because I was using my own energy instead of being a channel. It was such a scary feeling that I did not forget to detach again. I had no intention of picking up anyone's headaches, coughs, fears or problems in the future.

CONCEPTS

Energy transferences work because matter is not just solid and dense. It is a pattern of energy. Atoms will dissolve into energy patterns when broken down. Dynamic energy is not bound so heat is a form of energy. There is a fundamental interconnectedness of all matter, so everything is constantly affecting each other and all life. Mind, body, and emotions cannot be separated as one aspect must interpenetrate the other two. All living things have a tendency toward order. Health is in alignment with order. Disease is misalignment and not natural. Within each individual, there is a growth urge to become self-fulfilled. Touch stimulates that natural impulse and allows the person to self-heal by supplying the energy necessary to boost that person's system. That individual can then heal quicker as the energy goes to the parts that are deficient and creates a natural alignment towards health.

✷ ✷ ✷

BENEFITS OF TOUCH

Therapeutic Touch effects a relaxation response; it helps to alleviate and eradicate pain; and usually accelerates the healing process. It works well with stress-related diseases and has a significant effect on the autonomic nervous system such as slowing down brain waves, heat rate, and lowering blood pressure and pulse rate. It is used to balance energy and therefore is great in calming down colicky and irritable babies.

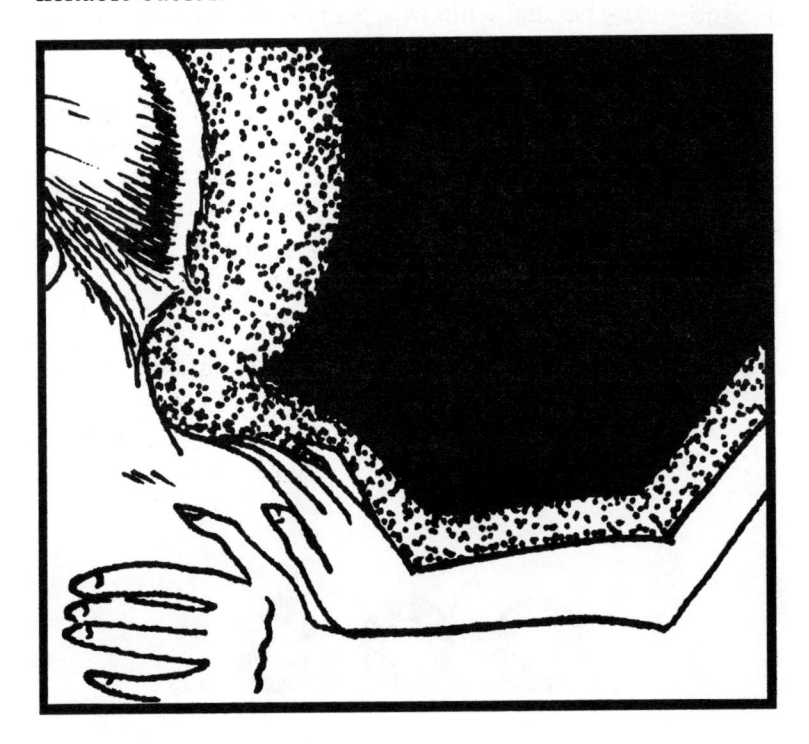

CHARACTERISTICS OF COLORED LIGHT

Every color is an energy frequency. It has been scientifically proven that emotions and feelings also have their own frequencies. Since colors and emotions can ride on the same wave length, a color has certain indigenous qualities all of its own. The following are qualities associated with these specific colors and will help you in your healing.

Red—is associated with love, basic instinct and survival.

Orange—energizing. Orange stimulates cells.

Yellow—mental acuity. Yellow is used when the mind needs more activation.

Green—healing. Green is the healing color utilized for any kind of healing; mental, physical or emotional.

Blue—calming. Blue is a relaxing frequency.

Purple—spirituality, purpose. Purple is spiritual and also allows you to see your purpose and what it means.

White—contains all of the above characteristics. When in doubt, use the white light as the person will absorb whatever frequencies are needed.

PROCESS OF THERAPEUTIC TOUCH

CENTERING

Relaxation or breathing techniques allows one to physically and psychologically find an inner sense of peace and stability. Visualize a bright luminescent beam of white light entering through the top of your head, going straight down your body, and out the bottom of your feet. These methods produce a natural shield and a protection for you so that you do not draw the patient's symptoms within you. This allows you to detach, yet empathize with the patient. When you center, you become a channel and you can then utilize the universal energy which is always available. Never utilize your own energy or you will feel depleted.

Once you have centered yourself, the client sits on a chair that has no back, or sideways on a chair that does have one. State an affirmation saying, "You wish the energy that is pulled through you to be for the best interest of the patient." You have just given intentionality to what you expect of the energy. Energy just "is." The person using it must be the one to determine what it is to be used for. Voodoo was a healing art used for making the sick, well. Some people started using it for evil and it become known as black magic. Everything positive can also be used for negativity. There are centering exercises at the end of this chapter that show you how to become a channel for the energy to pass through you to the patient.

ASSESSMENT

This phase is for gathering data about the patient. Retrieve information about how his voice sounds; what his posture looks like while walking, standing and sitting; observe facial affectations; note voice intonations and the fluidity of his bodily parts. Jot down these observations.

After the client is seated, stand next to him facing his profile so that you can easily put one hand six inches in front of his body and one hand six inches behind him. You will start to assess his electro-magnetic field in this fashion. While you are standing with one palm facing his forehead and the other palm facing the back of his head, move both of your hands symmetrically down his body until you get to his feet. You are looking for differences within his electro-magnetic field. These differences may come in various parts of the patient's body or deviations from the sensations felt from one hand to the other as you scan him. This may feel like heat, cold, tingling, pressure, whirling, pulsations, congestion, etc. Do not analyze what it means now; just notice where it occurs. Refer to the exercise section to learn how to feel an energy field between your hands. You are looking for differences in the person's energy flow. Although you are sensitizing yourself to changes in this flow, you are not making a medical diagnosis.

UNRUFFLING

When scanning a patient's field, the healer may feel pressure. This can mean congestion of the energy flow. Acupuncture is used to open these meridian lines to create the flow of energy to the vital organs, muscles and tissues. Touch has the same results by using energy transfers.

When you unruffle a patient's field, you do the same gestures as in the assessment phase, but you are not looking for anything. You do a downward sweep from the top of his head to the feet. When you get to his feet, sweep your hands away from his body. This unruffling of the energy field frees up any stagnated energy and gets it moving again. The healer can shake his hands to get rid of any excess energy when the sweep is finished. This sweeping act can mobilize the patient so that self-healing can start.

ENERGY TRANSFERENCE

When a person is healthy, she is a free flowing battery with no constrictions. There is an influx and output of energy that is exchanged within a person's field from the universal energy that the person can tune into. When an individual is deficit of energy, the healer is as powerful as her ability to direct, and modulate the frequency rate that she can pull through her. This bolsters the deficit of energy in the diseased individual. The energy that the client absorbs is instantly sent to areas that need healing. The healer must be balanced and centered mentally, physically, and emotionally to be effective. Nutrition and exercise play a large part in the health of the healer.

As a 220 line cannot be put into a 110 socket, a healer cannot process a frequency that is too powerful for her body to handle. To be effective and powerful as a healer, one must have all aspects of her being strong and balanced.

When a person is ill, a deficit of energy can be felt in his field as heat, cold, tingling, etc. The sickness is due to an imbalance of energies. The energy transference makes the ill person's field symmetrical once again. The assessment tells the healer where there are differences in the electromagnetic field. The healer then goes through the same process as in the assessment and the unruffling, only now the energy is pulled through the healer by visualizing white light going through her body and then transferring it to the patient. The patient automatically absorbs the healing light and utilizes it where it is needed. As the healer symmetrically runs her hands down the front and back of the person's field, she automatically transfers the energy and notes the differences in the field. Do this again for a second and third time and then assess how the client's field has changed from the assessment to the present. The healer should always think of wholeness and balance while transferring energy. Although the various colors can be processed to the healee for the illness, it is best for the novice to always send white light to allow the patient's body to draw upon the frequencies that are needed.

STOPPING

Knowing when to stop is the last phase. Energy is transferred immediately. If the energy is working, there are parasympathetic responses which can include a rumbling of the stomach, slower breathing, color comes into the face, the voice level goes down, and the shoulders drop. After the treatment, it takes twenty minutes for the energy to assimilate throughout the person's body. The client should stay still, lie down or sit quietly for that time period. A session with a child can last 7-10 minutes. An adult can last for 15-20 minutes. The healer definitely should stop if the patient starts fidgeting and can't sit still, if the voice level gets higher and faster, and if the client starts getting impatient. Then there is an energy overload. There are no harmful results, but be aware of the fact that the energy boost has reach its capacity for the present time.

Since touch speeds up the healing process, note that the symptoms can intensify before getting better. A cough may get much worse, temperature higher, and congestion can seem ten-fold. Since time is sped up, everything runs its course faster and much more intensely, but then the client can get better in half the amount of time. Let the client know this before he panics.

Depression and other emotional disorders can cause a suppression of the body's natural defenses against illness. This immuno-incompetence can later become translated into physical illness through an increased susceptibility to viral and bacterial agents as well as through internal sources of disease like cancer cells. Distortions originating at the etheric levels take time to work their way down to the physical level. It may be weeks or months before changes in the emotional and mental constitution manifest as physical illness. If the patterns of behavior can be changed, there is a chance that the illness will not crystallize into physical form. Then the path to illness could be reversed and homeostasis could be resumed.

When I first started practicing on others, I looked for anyone who was ill so that I could try this method. My friend had a cough and by the time I finished my great healing, he was coughing so badly that he thought he had to die to get better. Although he was much better the next day, he was real upset as I had forgotten to tell him that it was normal for the symptoms to intensify before he would feel relief. He became really frightened and thought that the treatment had made him worse. Make sure you tell your patients first so that fear doesn't set in. Be especially careful that you don't overload children with energy as you don't want them to be uncomfortable.

DISRUPTING DISEASE

It is said that the frequencies of an illness can be detected in an individual's electro-magnetic field for up to six months before manifesting themselves as physical symptoms. Therefore, if the behavioral patterns of the person can be changed, the electro-magnetic field would be comprised of higher, stronger vibrations. The result would be that these weaker frequencies would no longer manifest into the physicality of the person. The progression toward disease can be interrupted through the use of meditation and relaxation techniques. While drugs can interfere with the mechanisms of disease, they don't deal with the causes, although they can alter the expression of chronic disease. Meditation can disrupt the immune system and boost it to higher vibrations toward health. A trained individual can shift into a pattern of decreased sympathetic arousal. Relaxation increases stability in the autonomic nervous system of which the functions include the brain waves, heart rate, muscle tension, body temperature, stomach acidity and even the white blood cell levels.

✦ ✦ ✦

THE BRAIN

It is important to have access to both hemispheres of the brain as each hemisphere allows us to utilize more of our capacity for functioning at higher levels. The left hemisphere controls our reasoning, linear thinking, our five senses, motor and body movements, and a memory bank for about 24 hours (at that time the memory is shifted over to the right side of the brain). The right hemisphere controls the emotional, the unconscious, the hypothalamus (which controls the autonomic nervous system), the intuitive, the immune system, the long term memory bank, lymph nodes (contain defenses for diseases), and the creative aspects (such as art, music, cooking). Most of us live a majority of our lives using much more of our left brain. In order to center, relax and control the autonomic nervous system, we must be able to shift over to the right side. For long term memories and to get to our unconscious, the pathways to these two hemispheres are through using meditation, breath and relaxation techniques.

✦ ✦ ✦

CREATIVE ENERGY

Creative energy is passive. You mold it according to your thoughts, pictures and feelings. Your unconscious mind works from knowing the end result and uses the information stored in the mind and body. With your pictures, thoughts, and feelings, you set causes into motion that produce effects: jobs, relationships, possessions and even your health. These situations then reinforce the belief systems you hold in your consciousness. Your unconscious brings you what you have stored in your energy field. Meditation and centering brings this energy into your conscious awareness. The body is a place that every thought, emotion and memory call its home. The reason you bring about the future that you want is because you are the metabolic product of your experiences. All things are patterns of living energy. Information is processed and responded to.

HOLOGRAPHICS

Some scientists advocate the holographic concept which states that a single cell carries within it the capability to reproduce the entire adult structure. Since a person is considered a hologram, the entire whole is contained in every cell, and as a result, healing is a mutation of consciousness. As every cell changes, consciousness instantaneously changes. Conditioned patterns are constantly being triggered into conditioned responses. You have approximately sixty thousand thoughts a day. Repattern the thoughts if you want different results and consciously condition health, strength and well-being. The mind is not localized and every cell thinks. To reiterate, we are holographic focal points in a unified energy field.

REPLICATING CELLS

Ninety-eight per cent of all atoms are replaced every year. It takes three months to replace the skin, one month for the kidneys and less than two years to replace the entire body—every cell. In fact, eight million blood cells die in a healthy human adult every second. Since cells duplicate themselves exactly, a healthy cell replicates health. When stress and unbalance is present, the cells can mutate a bit, and that is what is replicated. When there is enough change in the cells, illness is created. A tumor that is viewed in an x-ray is not the same tumor that is seen six months later as it could have been replicated several times since the first viewing. It still remains a tumor if that is what is being duplicated. As the system gets stronger, the cells start to permeate toward health; the cell structure changes to its normal shape, and health is becoming restored.

HEALERS

Many studies have been conducted to find out the healing powers of healers. When healers held water and charged it, plants that were watered with it grew much taller than the controlled group of plants. When depressed individuals held regular water and fed it to plants, it resulted in a retarded rate of plant growth (compared to the control group). Mechanical devices were hooked up to healer's hands to show the energy output. It proved to be 100 times that of a hand that was not a healer. It is theorized that healers accomplish their acceleration of the normal growth and healing processes of living organisms by speeding up the activities of the cellular enzymes. Whatever the enzyme used, the healers always caused changes in activity which would result in a push toward greater health and energy balance of the sick organism. This healing energy appears to have an almost innate intelligence in the way it can therapeutically distinguish what energies are needed for each particular type of healing. The direction of change in frequencies is consistent with greater health of the cell and organism. Depending on whether the enzyme is one that adds to the energy of the cell or depletes its metabolic resources, the healer is able to speed up or slow down the reaction rate. Healer's energies are similar to powerful magnetic fields.

EXERCISES

TESTING THE HUMAN ENERGY FIELD

Cut a wire hanger so that only two sides are left and they form a right angle. Now cut another wire hanger in the same manner. With each hand, pick up a hanger so that you are holding the short end of each hanger lightly in your hand. Keeping your elbows bent, keep the long end of the rods parallel to the floor and point them at an individual about 15 feet away. As you start walking toward the individual, the rods will start to separate as you get to the edge of his electro-magnetic field. This may start to happen about 3-6 feet away from that person or 10-15 feet away from a person who has just relaxed or meditated. Meditation creates an extension of the energy field. These wires can be used as dowsing rods to sense energy fields. This exercise allows you to actually see where the person's field ends. It also shows you how you can be entrenched in someone else's energy and not realize it. Being in another's field may change your mood as you have picked up their energy, and with it, their problems.

★ ★ ★

BREATHING TECHNIQUES

Normal breathing is 16-18 breaths per minute. The ideal is 11-13. The faster you breathe, the less you feel. At 26 breaths per minute you lose the capacity to feel pain. Blood heats up while feelings and bodily sensations disappear. Great feats of strength occur when a person is in this state—later strain and fatigue take over. A mother is in this condition when she lifts up a car that has run over her child. People may say that she is pumping adrenaline throughout her, but it is also the rapid breathing that has allowed this woman to have this type of superhuman strength.

Conversely, the slower you breathe, the more you feel. Ten breaths per/minute for five minutes clears the mind and cancels out inharmonious vibrations around you for about the next four hours.

At three breaths per/minute vibratory levels become subdued and harmonized so psychic perceptions like intuitions, premonitions, and inspirations come easily. Great achievements occur at this level.

Increasing inhalation time and capacity increase the intake of prana. Extending time in inhalation allows this energy to be completely separate from air stored in the solar plexus. Lengthening exhalation time makes more room for prana by releasing toxins and impurities. Deeper breathing improves oxygenation of the blood and more energy to every organ, endocrine gland, nerve, muscle, tissue and cell. The following breathing and relaxation exercises enable you to center yourself quickly for a higher level of functioning.

DIAPHRAGMATIC BREATHING

This type of breathing soothes and releases tensions. Relaxation calms body interference, mental chatter, and allows you the ability to function in the moment rather than being stuck in the past or future.

Place your hands under your rib cage with your fingertips touching. Inhale while sending the air down to your fingertips. As you feel your diaphragm expanding, your ribs and chest separate and your fingers come slightly apart. Inhale slowly to the count of four. As you do this, think of the breath as a vitalizing factor and reconfirm it by visualizing pure air going throughout you with every breath. Hold the breath to the count of four. Exhale to the count of eight. Your fingertips come back together again as your chest lowers. Visualize that all negativity, toxins and problems are released with this exhalation. Breathing in and holding the breath should be the same count, while the exhalation is double that amount. So the proportion is 4-4-8. When that becomes easy, increase the count to 5-5-10, then to 6-6-12 etc. The slower you breathe, the more beneficial it will be. This should not be used only as an exercise, but it should become your normal way of breathing.

REVERSE BREATHING

This is an active and controlled meditative breathing technique. By pushing energy up into the chest, neck and head areas, blocked passages will start flowing with energy once again.

Place your hands under your rib cage with your fingertips touching. Tightly pull in the abdomen so that your fingertips overlap. Hold the abdomen in as you inhale to the count of four. Feel the ribs and chest expand. There will be resistance as the breath pushes against the abdomen. Hold the breath to the count of four.

Exhale through the mouth with the tip of your tongue against the roof of your mouth (which creates a hissing sound), and push the abdomen out as far as you can. Your fingertips will separate, the ribs will come together as the chest lowers. The exhalation should be double the count of the inhalation—in this case it is to a count of eight. The inhalation can stay at a count of four, but try increasing the exhalation to a count between 16-32. This strengthens the organs and blasts any blockages in the upper areas of the body. It makes you a clearer channel enabling you to create and function better.

RELAXATION TECHNIQUES
INSTANT MEDITATIONS

1. Inhale deeply. Connect your thumb with the tips of your first two fingers. As you exhale, slowly focus on a spot and stare at it for two minutes while you continue to breathe. Autonomic functions (brain waves, heart rate, pulse rate etc.) will slow down as you continue to center.

2. As you breathe, concentrate on the sound of the breath as it goes through your body and as it leaves on the exhalation. The sound becomes its own meditation as it centers you. Do this for two minutes.

3. Close your eyes, breathe, and visualize your entire body as a beam of white light. Every breath becomes a new shaft of light entering you. Since the white light has all of the healing rays, you are raising your frequencies and become a stronger channel for healing yourself and others.

4. Close your eyes and visualize a ball of red light entering through the top of your head, going down through your body and out the bottom of your feet. Every organ, muscle, tissue and cell of your body will take in whatever characteristics of this color that is needed. Then do this with orange, yellow, green, blue, purple, and white.

Red: Love, basic instincts, survival, attraction
Orange: Vitalizer, energizer
Yellow: Mental acuity
Green: Healing
Blue: Calmness, peace, serenity
Purple: Spirituality, purposefulness
White: Contains the characteristics of all the colors.

When you imagine these colors going through you, your body will automatically pull into it the frequencies of what these colors represent and every cell will be rejuvenated with what it needs.

INTENSIFYING ENERGY FIELDS

Since everything has an energy field, any object's field can be intensified and then used as a healing tool to help a patient recover quicker. For example, a towel, blanket, shirt, a rock, bandage or even a piece of cotton can be used as an energy field to hasten healing.

Lay the object in one palm of your hand, and with the other hand, reach down toward the object until you sense its field. Then pull white light directly down through you and then out your hand to the object. You are magnifying the frequencies of the object. Putting this object on the afflicted area of the patient provides an electrical field so that the person can self-heal faster. Sports medicine doctors do virtually the same thing when they encase the hurt area with an Ace bandage that is laced with electrodes. These wires are then plugged into a socket and the client stays in this electrical field. Therapeutic Touch just bypasses the actual electrical socket and provides its own. Chiropractors use the ultra-sound machine for this same purpose of healing. We become the ultra-sound machine by centering, processing the light and transferring it to the person. A blanket or shirt can be electrified in this manner to allow healing to take place when it is worn. When a rock is intensified, it can be carried and placed, when necessary, on the affected area. Cotton or bandages can be put on wounds so that the area heals faster. The way Touch can be used is bountiful and your imagination can bring forth wonders in how to help others.

SHIELDING

Shielding is a protection technique. When you awaken in the morning, think about putting yourself in white light that is being pulled into you from the universal energy and surrounding you for three feet around. Mentally visualize that this energy is a protective shield and that only well-intentioned vibrations can penetrate. You are then automatically put into a safe environment. Another method of doing this is to visualize yourself encompassed in a cylinder that is open at the top. Again program that this shield will only permit high vibrations to enter through the top of this tube. The shield can be done at any time when you think you need it.

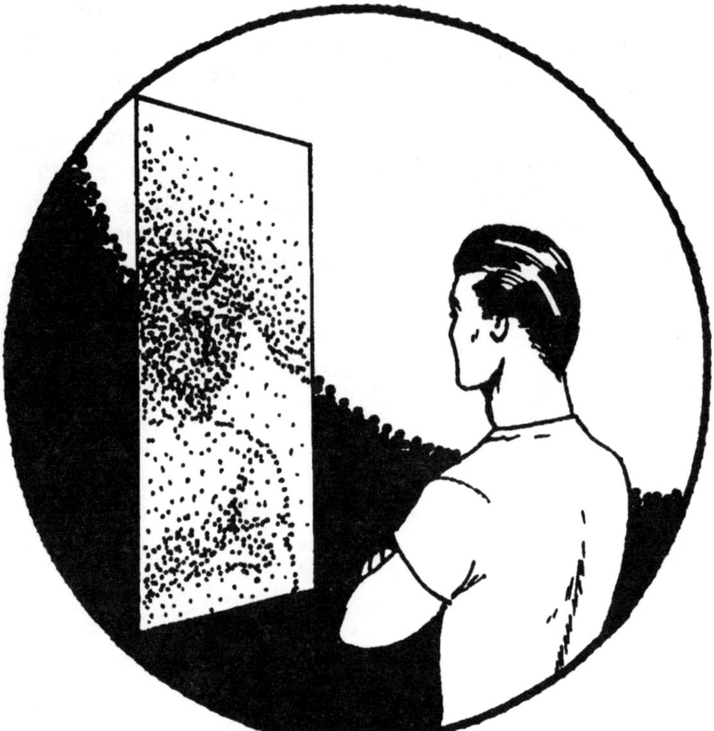

TIDBITS FOR EFFECTIVE LIVING

SPEAK TO YOUR BRAIN

The brain weighs less than three pounds and, in the adult, comprises less than 8.5% of our weight.

It is possible to "speak" directly to the brain and to exercise it. Oliver Wendell Holmes suggested that we could increase our brain use by thinking of ten impossible thoughts or to tell three outrageous lies.

We live in a rational world and our left hemisphere is far more developed because of it. We conceive of our brain as a thinking instrument that is essentially rational and logical. We have developed a whole series of programs to train the brain and we have put these types of programs into our educational institutions. We analyze Shakespeare's works instead of just feeling them. The S.A.T. tests are standardized tests that measure our intellect but they don't test the creative aspects of the person. By just merely showing the brain attention, more blood goes to the brain and oxygen goes with it. This stimulates the brain cells into rejuvenation and it can produce clearer, more effective thinking.

Your unconscious is like a computer and is programmed by your thoughts. Therefore, wrong-doing is only the result of wrong-thinking. If you don't like the results, you must change your thinking to produce the outcomes that you do want. It is said that we have a negative thought about ourselves every few minutes. Monitor your thoughts and make sure that you are reinforcing the positive traits that you want or you will be strengthening the negatives instead.

COMFORT VS. RISK

Most of us find it comfortable to stay in what we know best so we don't risk fear of failure. Risking allows us to reach another plateau and to be better in other ways. Risk at least once a day and you will find that you can do more than you ever thought you could do. Goals are really never meant to be reached. They just point you in a direction. When you have accomplished a goal, it is usually only a starting point to be, go, or to do something else. Therefore, what we consider an end result is really just another beginning. Without risking, we may never even find this starting point.

★ ☆ ★

EXCELLENCE

Practice does not make perfect. Only perfect practice makes perfect. Otherwise, you are perfecting something that you do not want. Make sure that the knowledge and the skills are down pat so that the correct method of execution can produce the goals that you are striving for.

SMILE, YOU'RE ON CANDID CAMERA

Make a list of all your wonderful character traits and hang it in a place that you pass by often. It is great for building self-esteem and when you are not feeling so wonderful, it serves as a pick-me-up. Laughing and singing is great for your mental health. When you smile, it is difficult to feel depressed. Walk away from your problem for a while and do something that makes you feel good. When you come back to that problem, it won't seem as big. At least 85% of all illnesses are stress-related or psycho-induced. Be aware of the stress triggers in your life. Build up your self-esteem by doing something everyday that makes you happy. You will think more clearly, act more efficiently and handle stress more objectively.

☺ ☺ ☺

SUCCESS

What the mind can conceive, the mind can achieve. Realize that you have no limitations. You can do and be anything you want if you have the credentials and the mind-set. Recognize your potential, stretch beyond your limits to a new plateau and go for it. The results will far exceed your expectations. You are responsible for your own pleasures, your own rewards, your own successes and your own failures. If you use failures as learning experiences, they no longer are failures. Just take responsibility for whatever happens since you are your own master.

CELLS THAT THINK

Our bodies are fields of ideas that make interpretations to the mind and the body simultaneously with no space-time differential. Your mind cannot be confined to one place and every cell of your body "thinks." By this I mean that if a person says he loves you, your mind and body react instantaneously. If you are in favor of that statement, the body will start producing the chemical Interferon, which creates an emotional high that we associate with the feeling of being in love; and the mind acts accordingly. If you don't like that statement, you may start producing adrenaline which is created in a fight or flight syndrome and the mind will react to that chemicalization which is indigenous to fright or fear. If you are thirsty, the entire being reacts simultaneously and not in a linear fashion. Valium is produced within the body when tranquillity is restored. These are just some examples as to how the mind/body connection works together.

✦ ✦ ✦

TRUTH OR FICTION

You create whatever you experience. Your interpretation of notions will translate into the biological events that follow. How we experience our body-space-time syndrome is our interpretation of such. We have developed time to explain the perception of change. No two people experience time the same way. Some people have a much faster internal perception of time and it is translated as "always running out of time, or there is never enough time, or time is of the essence." Others have a different interpretation as they have "too much time on their hands, time for everything, and more time to spare." Where do you fit in? Then realize the conditioned patterns that we respond to since we have approximately 60,000 thoughts a day. Only certain ones are reacted to. Make sure that they are the ones that are the most effective for you at that given time. Less than one billionth of the stimuli that we are bombarded with get into the nervous system. We consider that small percentage that is filtered through as reality. Changing what comes through that filter allows us to change our perspective about that given reality and will alter that opinion either slightly or all together. We are the metabolic product of our experiences since every thought, experience, and memory reside in our body. When we want to change an aspect of ourselves, it must be through a mutation of our consciousness to a different behavioral pattern.

GOAL SETTING

Visualizations of goals produce results when they are coupled with our strong positive feelings which are then backed by our energy. When we stretch our mind to new ideas, it will never go back to its original form. It is in this way that we create our own life. By effectively using all of your mental, emotional, and physical resources, you will magnetically draw to you whatever you need. You form this energy bond through your pictures, thoughts, images, behavioral patterns, feelings and your perceptions of your experiences. Your unconscious brings you what you have stored in your energy field. Every cell reproduces itself every eleven months. You produce a new body every two years. As your thoughts are of youth, health and beauty, your reproducing cells become more whole and perfect. As you repeat positive statements, they go down into the unconscious level and take form in the body. The body then expresses a positive attitude and that type of energy pattern is what the person then attracts to himself. Since creative energy is passive, you mold it according to your thoughts, images and feelings. Your unconscious mind works from knowing the end result. It uses this information which is stored in the mind and body to set causes into motion that will produce the desired effects: this is regarding such things as your job, house, relationship, health, etc. These situations then reinforce the belief systems you hold in your consciousness.

PRIORITIES

In order to get what you do want, deny what you don't want. This puts a stop order on unwanted conditions by declaring that they are finished. Release an emotional attachment to a situation or person that is no longer beneficial in your life. It is necessary to let go of the past in order to do something different in the future. When you take something away, something else is always going to fill it. Be cognizant of what is taking its place and make sure that it is strengthening you.

Many times people think they are *feeling* their feelings while they are merely *thinking* their feelings. Be aware of how you want to feel and be able to switch gears when it is not to your liking. Before you manage your energy to create something, know what it is you want. Get a picture of what you want to manifest. Once you choose your goal and set cause into motion, direct your unconscious mind to think positively about the goal. As you think of what you do want, clean out your thoughts and give up old images if they no longer suit you. Be flexible so that you can change easily to what is best for you in this present moment or you may be cemented into the past with goals that are no longer effective for the present time. This way you can create each day the way you want it to be and leave the past behind.

INTERNAL RHYTHMS

The most important external cue leading to the establishment of biological rhythms is light. Strong light is now accepted as one cue that may entrain or modify our internal rhythms. Most of us are not conscious of the intrinsic rhythms of our daily temperature, eating and sleeping patterns. Many short-term activity rhythms are phase-linked to eating and metabolic demands. Our usual rhythms of wakefulness and sleep center around twenty four hours and seem to exert a stabilizing effect on our physical and psychological health. A disruption in this rhythm results in different body rhythms. Jet lag partially explains the internal clock "remembering" back home time. Since the brain operates on a 25 hour rather than a 24 hour cycle, it is more natural to conform to a schedule that calls for the worker to shift forward in a work shift rather than backward. For instance, an 8:00 a.m. to 4:00 p.m. schedule is best followed by change to a 4 p.m. to midnight, not 12:00 midnight to 8 a.m. as it is working with rather than working against the circadian rhythms.

BLAME

Blame is one sure way to stay in a problem. Understanding enables us to rise above the issue and take control. Many times our parents taught us the same beliefs that they were taught. If it isn't working for us, we blame ourselves as it was good enough for them and it *should* be fine for us. You are the only person who knows what is good for you.

Stop for a moment and catch your thought. What are you thinking right now? Since your thoughts shape your life, would you want what you are thinking at this moment to become true for you? Stay away from thoughts that create problems and pain. Instead, choose to think thoughts that nourish and support you. When there is a problem, there is not something to *do*; there is something to *know*. Take responsibility for your actions and stop blaming others or yourself for what is taking place. Just learn from the experience and grow.

PEACE AND CONTENTMENT

We must recognize contentment and peace and be able to stay in that state even when stressors are pulling on us from all directions. This involves being tuned into oneself and feeling the disturbances, but not adding to them and not denying them. Give yourself the space and time for things to settle back again. be aware of all the things you do which makes it difficult for you to regain your composure. Be cognizant of each moment and absorb it; do not react to or fight it. It is in the absorption that you can change moods. It is, "I am depressed. I recognize that feeling." and move on to another mood. When you can *feel* rather than *label* what you are feeling, then you can switch to something else that makes you feel better. Don't give names to experiences, but just note if that energy is compatible with you. Sometimes confusion is good as it allows for change to take place. When you don't *know* what is going on, you are forced to *be* with what is going on. Then you are living in the moment. At that time you do not have to practice awareness, you *are* self-aware.

WINNERS VS. LOSERS

Knowing how to use verb tenses can be a powerful aid in communication. Adding "ing" to the verb makes it into a moving image in your mind. For instance, "I was running to her." has more action than what could be considered a still picture in your mind of "I ran to her." If you want to disassociate from the past, use the simple past tense of the verb. If you want to associate and feel more of the action, add the "ing" to the verb. This can put you directly into the mental attitude of how you were feeling then. If you are depressed, use this technique to think of something in the past that made you happy, proud and feeling strong. Consolidate that past picture into one sentence and use the "ing" in the verb tense to shift your mood swing into the present. "I am *feeling* stronger as I was proud of my speech." is an example of bringing the past into the *now*.

If you have a problem and you want to disassociate from it, place it in the far distant past by using the past perfect tense of the verb: "*I had been angry* with her." this shows a completion in your thoughts and allows you to then go on with your life. When you have acknowledged completion in a certain area of your life, you will react differently. When your responses change, the reactions of others will also change in regard to you.

Realize that your verb tenses can shift your attitude as to how you feel about the situation. "I'm amazed at how much trouble it *caused* me" is a different connotation than using the verb *causes* in that sentence. Listening to yourself makes you become aware of what incidents are still creating stress for you and which are actually in completion.

A cause must always exist earlier than an effect. People who are powerful feel themselves as *causes* with choices and this motivates them into action. Those who feel helpless perceive themselves as *effects*. Those who have high self-esteem will view stresses as challenges and be motivated by them. Others with less esteem will play the part of the victim and allow these stressors to overcome them. Think of the cause-effect beliefs that you hold as true. "Germs cause disease. Loving your child will make him a balanced adult. Suffering is good for your soul."

The first step is to be aware that you have these beliefs, then analyze which ones you still wish to keep, which are no longer valid, and change those to beliefs that are more beneficial for you now. <u>Problems are merely patterns that have not been updated. Nothing has any meaning until you assign a meaning to it.</u> Just take an inventory of what views are meaningful to you and if they are resourceful in your life. People usually justify and defend their behaviors. This is fine just as long as they are open to new behaviors that may be more suitable.

CLEAR THINKING

Thinking too much about yourself can keep you from knowing what you want in the present, as you are too caught up in the past and in what the future may bring. You must make a distinction between your understanding and the terms in which your understanding is expressed. Your belief systems are not your understanding but your vehicles of expression. You create new models every time you have a better understanding of what you are creating, how, and why. These modalities are all subject to change as you change or you will be using outmoded methods to solve present day situations. Your interpretation of the facts stand between you and your clarity of perception.

✦ ✦ ✦

THE ENERGIZER

Do not energize past-oriented guilt and future-oriented fear. Past experiences are not comprehensive enough to provide a basis for understanding everything in the present. We give them credibility and authority. If we are still looking at an experience through the feelings of a situation from childhood, we will be viewing it with a child's perception and still validating it in adulthood. You are where your attention takes you. *You are your attention.* Notice when hesitation and procrastination persists as it could be an indication of a continued trust in fear and reason. Remember, risking stretches us to new levels and more opportunities. The more clearly you see the future you desire, the more likely it will come true.

✸ ✸ ✸

SHIFTING MOODS

When things are not going as planned, when we are frustrated, or all of our efforts seem to be for naught, hopelessness could be the outlook at the moment. At this time we have become part of the problem and need a method to shift our attitude and to be able to look at things differently. At these times, nothing sounds like fun and wallowing in pity takes hold. For this reason, make up a list of fun activities and utilize at least one of these things on a daily basis. Even when you don't feel like taking time out for fun—DO IT! Your entire attitude will change and you will feel better about coping. To overcome something means you must objectively discover the real cause of the disturbance. This will allow you to create what you want instead.

The creative process is simple. Write down the things and the conditions that you want; read the list daily and make any necessary changes. Know that it will happen. Act and think about it as if you have it already. Remain open and flexible to any other changes as they come your way. You will never know what you could do or what you could become if you don't try.

UNLIMITED POWER

We have unlimited power. Creating what we want is a matter of identifying with your power, understanding its characteristics and learning to use it effectively. When a child is born, its thoughts and feelings are limitless because its mind is in a clear slate. Children attempt the impossible, unaware that they have any limitations. It is only later that they learn the confines of human expectancy. Although these boundaries are illusions, they gain validity and eventually the concepts become physical reality. It's as if all these people have predetermined what you will experience. Let every moment produce the future you desire as you deserve it.

BEHAVIOR VS. FEELINGS

Behavior is sometimes thought to be more important than feelings. We could grow up stifling our feelings in order to act correctly. The symptoms caused by that behavior will be sure to show up negatively at some point. It is *how* we respond to what happens that is important—not *what* has actually happened. Someone could tell us that we are beautiful, but that has no meaning unless we actually believe and internalize it.

We must tend toward individuated maturity. That means that we have become our own person and don't need parental approval. Some people are still trying for this approval even though their parents have passed away. When we can base decisions on our own needs without guilt and anxiety, then we are growing up. It is important to learn how to do our own emotional comforting. It is as equally important to be able to give permission to others to be an individual, even if it is not to our liking. Just let them know you are there for them, are listening to them, and that they are understood.

A parent's evaluation is valid to the child as it is the only source of who and what they are from birth. If this child is called lazy, selfish and inconsiderate, we are reinforcing that attitude and the set of behaviors that go along with it. What is wrong can be pointed out, but there is also a need to know what is right. Everyone needs appreciation, not depreciation. We tend to forget to show appreciation because we only remember the bad things. Eliminate depreciation by describing the good character traits of the individual and building up self-esteem. Then a set of positive behavior starts to show up instead.

SWITCHING EMOTIONS

A person usually elicits the same set of behaviors in similar situations. He can identify with himself because he has had these symptoms for a long time. If another package of behaviors come out under similar circumstances, an initial comment may be, "I am not myself today." We generally treat emotions as something that comes and hits us. For example—an anxiety attack. No behavior is compulsive unless it is done 24 hours a day, every day. If a person is not doing this behavior some of the time, then it can be lessened or eliminated.

Emotions contain information that is valuable to us. Analyzing these emotions uncovers our perspectives about the situation or the people that we allowed to "get to us." Many times emotions have a time frame. Guilt is associated with the past, and ambition is future oriented. Change the time frame and the emotion will start losing its hold on you. Guilt requires a comparison of what happened—to a fantasy of what could have happened. When you abolish the comparison, it then just becomes a recollection. Guilt also shows your that you have standards for your behaviors. Anger happens when your value system is threatened or violated. Different people going through the same exact experiences can go through very different emotions depending upon their standards, value system and their perspective of it. When you are feeling a particular emotion, recognize what you are saying to yourself and how your body feels (what part tightens up). Then think of the time you felt joy and how your body reacted to that emotion. Now you have a comparison.

Duplicate that joyous feeling when you want to switch out of a state of being that you don't want to be in.

CONDITIONING

Individuals will react differently even when the same set of stimuli is presented. Example—Two children are making a mess in the kitchen. The mother comes in and spanks both of them and calls them bad children. This is the raw experience. The first child may focus on the fact that he is bad, that he hurt his mother, that the world is unpredictable, he is dumb, and that he can't handle things well. The second child can focus on the fact that his mother doesn't like a dirty kitchen, he is likely to get spanked if he does things that his mother does not like, there are plenty of other places outside to make a mess, that the world is unpredictable and he is capable of handling it.

Both of these children had the same exact stimuli and both experienced it totally differently. It is the matter as to whether you view a partially filled glass of water as half full or half empty. We constantly create opinions and instead of reacting freely to them, we rely on similar past experiences and usually react the same way as before even if it is not beneficial. Even old opinions that are no longer effective offer security because we are used to them and we are generally a creature of familiarity and habit. We will never have positive changes unless the desire to alter our circumstances is greater than the comfort of familiar pain.

The past no longer exists; only your memory of it does. As your opinions change, so do the memories and reactions to those memories. Past incidents are relatively unimportant. When our opinions are changed, the memory of the incident remains; but the effect on us is altered. The future grows out of our present thoughts. We have the ability to change these thoughts to what is powerful for us now. Success is a skill and it takes proper practice to become an expert.

Condition yourself to redirect ideas to positive notions and attitudes. Consider that new job as a challenge instead of an impossibility, that new move as an adventure instead of a burden, and that unknown future as a fabulous movie script instead of a psycho-drama.

Detach from great emotional situations by saying, "I am *feeling* angry," instead of "*I am* angry." The difference in semantics allows you to step away from this anger and makes it a separate entity from you.

Reaffirm suggestions that empower you. Keep repeating suggestions until your mind and body act accordingly. If you keep telling yourself you don't feel well—you won't. Keep reinforcing what you do want instead. Give yourself orders that you want carried out and it will be natural to do so. Put yourself into situations with the types of people you want to be with and the energy of this will become familiar and attractive to you.

It is all a matter of conditioning yourself and your environment as to what you want and need for the moment. This is a determining factor for your future. Create your future by taking care of yourself now.

DYNAMICS OF CHANGE

The action you take produces your outcome. The first step is to state what it is that you want as an outcome. You then have various possibilities to reach it. The next step is to choose which directions might produce the desired results and then take action. The action then results in the outcome. If the results do not match your original goal, you have choices. Try again or consider yourself a failure and go into a negative spiral of not trying. If you take the positive approach, learn why it didn't work, gather more knowledge about the subject, and try again. Your self-confidence level will increase. If you take the negative course of "I can't do it," then you will not be growing or gaining from the experience. It is easy to not make mistakes when the tasks are familiar. Then you become a winner because the success ratio is high. It is more difficult to risk when the circumstance is not familiar and the chance of not doing well and failing is high. It is only in the risking that growth comes about. This is where new information is learned and can be applied. Otherwise you are always using what you already know.

BELIEF SYSTEMS

An affirmation is a statement of word, thought, feeling, symbol, image or action which confirms a belief pattern that you hold. Every thought you have about life goes to fruition to create the events that are your future. The future is all around you as you attract and draw the situations that match and reflect your inner thoughts.

It is really a process of awareness. If you want to buy a red sports car, you would notice every red sports car on the road and this may enforce your desire. I may be oblivious to these cars as it is not in my thinking pattern. If I want a coat, I would see what is new and what styles are appealing. Coats may hold no interest for you—they would just be another item in the store. What we need is always around. Our reality is manifested by where we pay attention.

You are made up of billions of beliefs that are learned since birth and added to every day. These beliefs concern your body, intellectual worth, attractiveness, mortality, family, society, government, life after death and so on. These are your own truths and your mind holds on to them with great determination. Circumstances may have changed and the belief patterns may not have. This means that you may be holding on to beliefs that are no longer valid or beneficial. Growth and maturity come with flexibility and change. At the point where you have so much confidence in your truths you can stand alone and change whatever is necessary to create what you want. This growth also comes when you work through the troubled areas in your life. It is not how *long* you live, but the quality of *how* you live.

Our outer world reflects what is going on inside. If you are a positive person, that is what you will attract. If you are a mess inside, your outer world will show it. The mind likes limitation and familiarity—that is what it is used to. Change becomes scary, it is an unknown; yet *you will never know what you may have and become if you don't try.*

PROCESS FOR CHANGE

Repetitive affirmations, prayers, or chants are great for your health as the repetition alone slows down all of your bodily processes and makes you feel better. As the repetition becomes ingrained within you, change becomes easier.

Review a past success and use this as an anchor for further successes. Build a "success mentality", affirming that your present and future events will be as rewarding. We have many successes each day and tend to underplay or ignore many of them. When you see your life as important, each act, however small, becomes important as well.

Choose people and places that strengthen your energy.

Society constantly dictates what is right and what is wrong. It is not to our advantage to buy into some of these statements: "It can't work. It's not possible. You are not allowed." These thoughts are repeated many times throughout our lifetime. Then if things don't materialize, the mind can say it didn't expect it anyway and we adjust our expectation to accommodate these disappointments. When other people's energies are low, they pull on us for support. This is fine as long as you are not pulled out of control. Many times we are pulled by the emotional manipulations of others. They can come in the guise of duty, honor, need, fear, or obligations to get us to succumb to their will. Once you realize this, you can come to your own decisions even if those decisions are unpopular.

To reach any goals, don't make promises you can't keep. As you become true to your word, your thoughts begin to manifest themselves. If you say things just to appease others, you don't expect your conscious thoughts to be reality, and they won't be. As your thoughts and words become more powerful, the energy attached to them increases. When this is coupled with action, the result is a quick shifting from a conscious stream into reality as there is nothing to clutter the delivery system.

FACTS AND OPINIONS

Emotionality gives intensified power to the belief system. Whatever you firmly believe in will hold more power for you. Affirm positive power by laughing at your weaknesses. Each moment programmed information is added to the contents that are already laid down within your system of beliefs. You have the choice of affirming either the negative or positive thought patterns as they bombard you.

If you have had a negative experience, write down what actually occurred and what you learned from it. If you can't come up with an answer, then you didn't get the message and the lesson will come again in another form.

Your thoughts are empowered by the vitality and quality of your energy. This vitality is expressed through your emotions. As you express emotions, the feelings around you change and consequently the reality you draw is rearranged by your energy shift. If the emotion is anger, your body will start acting adversely and your ability to control events is lost. You now consider yourself a victim of circumstance. By calming your emotions, your thoughts can grow and you will see things as they are, rather than the inaccurate opinions of before. *Facts are*! Your perspectives of these facts are your opinions. By shifting your views and getting balanced, your opinions will also change.

We must also recognize that there can be a split as to what we feel inside and what we show the outside world. If there is too much of a difference, an imbalance is created and a dichotomy is formed. This can bring disturbances within as we are trying to be someone we are not. By accepting who we are, we can go on to better things and gain footholds in this dimension. Our thought forms should be slightly beyond where we are now so it becomes a new plateau to strive for.

Concentrate on what you want, and go for it. This energizes your will power and allows you to move into the right place at the right time. If you don't know what you want, clear out what you know you definitely no longer want, so what is left becomes clearer.

Be consistent in your thoughts once you have decided what you do want. Feel that it has already happened. This thought is then put into your reality and keeps your intentions clear. Concentrate on little steps to reach your goals rather than the whole picture. Desires or needs are contributing factors to the intensity of where you put your attention; although needs are easier to fulfill than desires. The reason for that is because a need is generally a necessity (shelter, food, clothing), and we are motivated to accomplish whatever tasks necessary to have these needs met as soon as possible. Desires are usually luxuries that we could live without, although they would be nice to have. Because they are not life threatening, it is not as motivating for us as a "need" is.

PRESENT TIME

Thoughts you have exist in the present time frame. You may think about a future event, image it, and feel great about it; but it is not reality, as it is an event in consciousness *about* reality. Time is a measure of consciousness. You want your affirmations to materialize in the future, even if that is only three minutes away. If you think about the future, it is not the "future", it is the present inventing a possible future. You may image the most perfect day for a picnic; yet if it rains, your visualization will probably need an alternative plan. NOW is the only reality. The relationship between your thoughts and the material world is vital. Outside the mind, the perspective of things may differ. A red flower in a garden is not red unless you perceive it as such; to an animal, it would be a colorless form; if nothing was there to see it, it would be just molecules moving about.

Create a well defined intention and put it in an undefined time frame. The more specific you are with your intentions, the more powerful the results. If you concentrate on a problem, all your thoughts will be engaged by that problem and you will gradually solidify its reality while eliminating the input of any other energies. Then the solution comes from what you believe since that is the only reality you can perceive at that time.

AWARENESS

When you experience mood swings, watch when your feelings begin to deteriorate and correct them. If you become grumpy when you are tired, don't make decisions at that time.

Play and laughter are the first things that go when illness or depression occurs because both play and laughter are considered a waste of time. Play can be considered any activity that produces the emotion of joy or that produces the experience of having fun.

When you are in a depressed mood and need fun the most, nothing sounds great. This is one reason why it is advisable to make a list of all the things that you enjoy doing and that give you pleasure. Create this list when you are feeling fine. Then do one of these activities daily for at least 1/2 hour a day. This is your time for yourself. When you are having a rough day, still maintain this play schedule as it will shift your attitude away from your problem. Then you can objectively view it without being part of the problem. Play creates healing as you can't have fun and be depressed. Playing breaks up the depression, while the laughter promotes the increase of endorphins within you which also promotes health.

BE TRUE TO YOURSELF

If you devote your effort to those things which are suited to you, you are in keeping with your true character and have found your calling. By applying your concentration to those things, you will sense the value of your work and the value of your life. There is no calling when you don't make the effort, but creative progress increases when you carry out what you like best.

You are generally good at the things that you like and progress seems to come easy. It is usually difficult to concentrate on things that you don't like, and consequently progress is slow because the state of mind and body are not unified.

Energy has both positive or plus poles, as well as negative or minus modalities. When we are positive, we feel strong. A positive life depends on a positive attitude. If it gets windy and you think that you can catch a cold, your attitude and energy have become negative or in the minus modality. When you think that wind can't bother you, it won't, and the energy is maintained on the plus side. Many people set out with the idea of a positive approach, but some form of negativity quickly defeats them. Both plus and minus thinking methods apply to everything. For instance, a person might see his bosses talking together. The person with a plus attitude will think nothing of it. The person with a minus attitude will immediately wonder if they are saying something bad about him.

While some people will put a bad interpretation on some words, others would put a good one on the very same words. The same words could sound differently to the same person depending on whether his attitude is plus or minus when he hears them. Remember, like energies attract one another. Therefore, plus attracts plus, and minus attracts minus. If you are in a minus frame of mind, you will think minus, do minus, and change everything around you to minus. Because minus calls minus, if one thing goes bad, everything will look bad unless you center yourself, neutralize your energy, and return to plus energy and attitude. Negative energy is powerful enough to change other people's energy to a minus mode if they allow it.

On the contrary, if your energy is plus, your thoughts, deeds, and everything around you will be plus also. A person with a strongly plus nature enlivens a group and can also change their attitudes for the better. A positive person becomes a great pick-me-up for anyone around.

When things are going well, anyone can easily keep positive, but we have to discipline ourselves to change negative to positive when conditions are adverse.

RELAXATION VS. TENSION

Humans cannot stand continuous tension. It is essential to be able to relax both the mind and the body when it is needed at any time and any place. When you relax properly, you are very strong and at your best. Most people don't know how to relax. If they relax their neck, the stomach tenses up and if they try to relax their stomach, another part tightens. This creates a constant tension somewhere at all times. By tensing yourself, you are interfering with your own strength and making things more difficult as your energy is constricted and not flowing properly throughout your body. Most people cannot relax in an emergency as they believe that relaxation means loss of power, when in essence, it is the strongest state you can be in. Relaxation techniques should be practiced until they are readily accessible for your use when you need them. A technique is of no use if it only works in a practice session. We must train ourselves, so that whatever happens, we can still maintain balance and coordination of our mind and body for total effectiveness.

MOOD CHANGERS

Every emotion that we feel is actually an energy frequency that is pulsating through us. Anger is a heavy, slow vibration; whereas happiness is a light, fast vibration. When anyone is angry or surprised, a faster pulse rate is generated. Calmness exudes a slow pulse rate. When we want to speed up our pulse all we have to do is concentrate deeply on being angry and it will increase. If we concentrate on a peaceful scene, our pulse rate will slow down. The difficult thing is not changing our pulse rate, but to freely change our mind. Conversely, when you want to access a different mood, breathe deeply, relax, and visualize a scene that makes you feel great. You will automatically slow down your heart rate, pulse rate, blood pressure and brain waves. This creates a calm feeling and a better attitude.

DEEP BREATHING

Concentrate on breathing from your abdomen and not from your chest which is considered shallow breathing. When your breath comes from a place around six inches below your navel, you have created a low, balanced center of gravity for yourself and a point to concentrate on for stability. When you are angry, breathe deeply into this point and the anger will dissipate as your mood changes. Though it is easy to direct your mind to do things that you like, and hard to direct it toward things that you do not like, practice this type of breathing with the one point below your navel. It will help you become more balanced.

We can manage to live for a time without eating, but if breathing stops for even a little while, we are dead. A healthy person breathes in long strong breaths; a sickly person breathes in short weak ones. When we are stable, our breath is quiet and even, whereas when we are nervous, we breathe randomly and in jerks. We can always promote stability and preserve health by controlling our breathing.

Basic human instincts are at the same level as animals. We consider a person to be inhuman if he does not live at a higher level than basic instincts because then he lacks the characteristic traits of humanity. A person who has gone completely berserk and has lost all reasoning becomes a thing. Although he maintains the outward form of humanity, he has lost humanistic characterizing traits.

CHANGING PERSPECTIVES

All things change according to the way we look at them. If we look at the creative developing side of the world situation, it seems to be harmonious. Looking at the death and destruction aspects lead us to believe this is a cruel world. If we want to create a nasty world and invite a miserable life, all we need to do is adopt a negative attitude and view everything through it. When you are negative, nothing will interest you and you will make no attempt to understand the bright side of situations. If your attitude is positive, you will be pleased and everything you see and hear will be pleasant. When we are aligned and balanced, we do not fight with our opponents to win or to lose. Both people can correct each others weak points, and through mutual respect, can help each other and both turn out winners.

☺ ☹ ☺

THINKING FOR HEALTH

Try this exercise. Pour water into a tub and stir it up. Then try to calm the water with your hands; you will only succeed in agitating it further. Let it stand undisturbed for a while, and it will calm down by itself. The human brain works much the same way. When you think, you set up brain waves. Trying to calm them down by thinking is only a waste. People who cannot sleep and lie awake thinking, are creating more turbulence until sleep is impossible. Again, do some deep breathing or visualize a peaceful scene and you will calm down.

SYMBOLS FOR GROWTH

Everyone has some kind of habits. We do not need to try to get rid of those that are harmless, but we should break ourselves of those that cause error, trouble, or unpleasantness. Many of these habits are learned patterns of behavior that are deeply seated in our unconscious and are difficult to access and to break. Each person who hears a word has a large store of unconscious material concerning it, and this material results in vastly differing interpretations of the word. The unconsciousness is the storehouse in which all of our knowledge and experience are stored. If our past experiences associated with that word, song, person, or symbol have been good ones, our association to it will be pleasant. A word or a picture is merely a symbol representing our experiences. Depending on how we have interpreted that symbol in the past, is how we generally relate to it in the present. An American flag is a symbol. If we have pride in America, we will have pride in the flag. A police siren stirs up all kinds of feelings. Some people will feel safe while hearing it and others will dread the sound. All of these symbols are traced back to our past experiences. The determining factors of how we feel about the symbol now depends upon whether our past associations with them were good or bad. Our present unconsciousness is a result of a long period of conscious suggestions from all of the things and circumstances around us. Changing the unconscious involves resolving your will power to take in only information that will help you and to reject everything else. If weak suggestions are repeated over a long period of time, it gains strength and that becomes your belief system.

RESPONSIBILITY

Whatever environment you come from, you must build your own personality. Each person is responsible for himself and has the means to become the best he can be. When you give in to negativity, your entire system becomes minus and you become weak. Don't buy into other people's belief systems. They may not work for you. Make sure that what you are accepting is for your best interest and that it benefits your purpose. What is not good for someone else may be positive for you.

When you get up in the morning, look in the mirror and say something positive to yourself. Do this every morning and strengthen what you need. Your confidence level will improve and you will be reinforcing the positive aspects.

Once you understand how you are affected by suggestions, be careful to use only positive words. Without knowing it, a carelessly spoken word can enter the unconscious. It is wrong to say such things as "I'm no good, " or "I can't," because you are then reinforcing the negative.

✧ ✧ ✧

CALMNESS AND POWER

As we sit still we imagine that we are in a state of complete calm, but within all of our calm includes much activity until we learn how to calm down our autonomic nervous system through relaxation techniques. Tops that children play with approach a state of calm stability the faster they spin. The top's most perfect state of calm is reached when it moves at the greatest speed. This is what is meant by action within calm. True calm is not merely sitting still and allowing your consciousness to grow vague. We must be able to instantaneously move with great speed and yet remain calm while doing so. By deeply breathing into the spot six inches below your navel, a calmness and stability will be maintained within. This stability will manifest itself as efficiency. We will then be able to handle whatever complexities that may come into our lives with a sense of ease.

✴ ✴ ✴

ABOUT THE AUTHOR

By helping others help themselves, Dr. Madeleine Singer has come full circle in her own search for the ultimate self. Her philosophy of Changing Ordinary to Extraordinary has served to make her a dynamic and effective educator for personal productivity and performance. Globally, she currently works with Fortune 500 Corporations, universities and groups of all sizes in the areas of creative thinking, stress management, productivity and effectiveness training, including relaxation techniques for transformational growth.

Born in New York and raised in Connecticut, she received her B.S. in Education with majors in science and psychology from Southern Connecticut State College; Dr. Singer is certified in Therapeutic Touch by the New York University School of Nursing and in Psychic Development by the Patricia Hayes School of Inner Sense Development. Her extensive training includes herbology, nutrition, acupressure and myotherapy, and she is experienced in Time Line Therapy. Dr. Singer is a practitioner of Neuro-Linguistic Programming with majors in education, health, creativity and leadership. She attained her Doctorate in Clinical Hypnotherapy through the American Institute of Hypnotherapy.

Dr. Singer has produced and hosted two television series, 'The Holistic Approach' and 'Energetix.' She is also a health columnist for several magazines and the author of two other books, *Insights* and *The Psychology of Synergy*.